CAMBRIDGE PRIMARY
Mathematics

4

Games Book

Emma Low

CAMBRIDGE
UNIVERSITY PRESS

CAMBRIDGE
UNIVERSITY PRESS

University Printing House, Cambridge CB2 8BS, United Kingdom

One Liberty Plaza, 20th Floor, New York, NY 10006, USA

477 Williamstown Road, Port Melbourne, VIC 3207, Australia

4843/24, 2nd Floor, Ansari Road, Daryaganj, Delhi – 110002, India

79 Anson Road, #06–04/06, Singapore 079906

Cambridge University Press is part of the University of Cambridge.

It furthers the University's mission by disseminating knowledge in the pursuit of education, learning and research at the highest international levels of excellence.

www.cambridge.org
Information on this title: www.cambridge.org/9781107685420

First published 2014

20 19 18 17 16 15 14 13 12 11 10 9 8

Printed in the United Kingdom by Latimer Trend

A catalogue record for this publication is available from the British Library

ISBN 978-1-107-68542-0 Paperback

Cover artwork: Bill Bolton

CD-ROM Terms and conditions of use

This End User License Agreement ('EULA') is a legal agreement between 'You' (which means the individual customer) and Cambridge University Press ('the Licensor') for *Cambridge Primary Mathematics Games Book Stage 4* CD-ROM ('the Product'). Please read this EULA carefully. By continuing to use the Product, You agree to the terms of this EULA. If You do not agree to this EULA, please do not use this Product and promptly return it to the place where you obtained it.

1. Licence
The Licensor grants You the right to use the Product under the terms of this EULA as follows:
(a) You may only install one copy of this Product (i) on a single computer or secure network server for use by one or more people at different times, or (ii) on one or more computers for use by a single person (provided the Product is only used on one computer at one time and is only used by that single person).
(b) You may only use the Product for non-profit, educational purposes.
(c) You shall not and shall not permit anyone else to: (i) copy or authorise copying of the Product, (ii) translate the Product, (iii) reverse-engineer, disassemble or decompile the Product, or (iv) transfer, sell, assign or otherwise convey any portion of the Product.

2. Copyright
(a) All content provided as part of the Product (including text, images and ancillary material) and all software, code, and metadata related to the Product is the copyright of the Licensor or has been licensed to the Licensor, and is protected by copyright and all other applicable intellectual property laws and international treaties.
(b) You may not copy the Product except for making one copy of the Product solely for backup or archival purposes. You may not alter, remove or destroy any copyright notice or other material placed on or with this Product.
(c) You may edit and make changes to any material provided in the Product in editable format ('Editable Material') and store copies of the resulting files ('Edited Files') for your own non-commercial, educational use, but You may not distribute Editable Materials or Edited Files to any third-party, or remove, alter, or destroy any copyright notices on Editable Materials or Edited Files, or copy any part of any Editable Material or Edited Files into any other file for any purpose whatsoever.

3. Liability and Indemnification
(a) The Product is supplied 'as-is' with no express guarantee as to its suitability. To the extent permitted by applicable law, the Licensor is not liable for costs of procurement of substitute products, damages or losses of any kind whatsoever resulting from the use of this Product, or errors or faults therein, and in every case the Licensor's liability shall be limited to the suggested list price or the amount actually paid by You for the Product, whichever is lower.
(b) You accept that the Licensor is not responsible for the persistency, accuracy or availability of any URLs of external or third-party internet websites referred to on the Product and does not guarantee that any content on such websites is, or will remain, accurate, appropriate or available. The Licensor shall not be liable for any content made available from any websites and URLs outside the Product or for the data collection or business practices of any third-party internet website or URL referenced by the Product.
(c) You agree to indemnify the Licensor and to keep indemnified the Licensor from and against any loss, cost, damage or expense (including without limitation damages paid to a third party and any reasonable legal costs) incurred by the Licensor as a result of your breach of any of the terms of this EULA.

4. Termination
Without prejudice to any other rights, the Licensor may terminate this EULA if You fail to comply with any of its terms and conditions. In such event, You must destroy all copies of the Product in your possession.

5. Governing law
This agreement is governed by the laws of England and Wales, without regard to its conflict of laws provision, and each party irrevocably submits to the exclusive jurisdiction of the English courts. The parties disclaim the application of the United Nations Convention on the International Sale of Goods.

Contents

Introduction

This Games Book consolidates and reinforces mathematical learning for Stage 4 learners (usually 8–9 years). It can be used as an independent resource for anyone wanting to encourage mathematical learning in children, or as a supplementary part of the *Cambridge Primary Mathematics* series.

If used as part of the series alongside the *Teacher's Resource 4* (9781107692947), then you will often be going directly to a specific game and page number according to the reference in the '*More activities*' section in the *Teacher's Resource* and will therefore already be familiar with the learning outcome of the game. If you are using the book as an independent resource, you can use the Objective map on the CD-ROM to help you determine what game you might want to play according to what learning outcome you are after, or you can simply read the '*Maths focus*' at the start of each game to decide if it's appropriate.

The games are grouped by strand, i.e. 'Number', 'Geometry', 'Measure' and 'Handling data' so that an independent user can easily navigate the pool of games. For those of you using this book alongside the *Teacher's Resource 4*, you will find that the games within a strand are ordered according to the order in which they are referenced in the *Teacher's Resource 4* (if you grouped all chapters of a given strand together).

Please note that the *Games Book* on its own does **not** cover all of the Cambridge Primary mathematics curriculum framework for Stage 4.

All games boards, game cards and record sheets provided within the printed book are also available on the CD-ROM for quick printing if preferred. Some games boards and resources will also be provided as Word documents so that you can adapt them as required. The CD-ROM also provides child-friendly instructions for each game, which can be displayed at the front of the class or sent home with the games for independent play. Nets for making dice, spinners and other useful mathematical resources are also provided as printable PDFs on the CD-ROM.

 This publication is part of the *Cambridge Primary Maths* project. *Cambridge Primary Maths* is an innovative combination of curriculum and resources designed to support teachers and learners to succeed in primary mathematics through best-practice international maths teaching and a problem-solving approach.

Cambridge Primary Maths brings together the world-class Cambridge Primary mathematics curriculum from Cambridge International Examinations, high-quality publishing from Cambridge University Press and expertise in engaging online enrichment materials for the mathematics curriculum from NRICH.

Teachers have access to an online tool that maps resources and links to materials offered through the primary mathematics curriculum, NRICH and Cambridge Primary mathematics textbooks and e-books. These resources include engaging online activities, best-practice guidance and examples of *Cambridge Primary Maths* in action.

The Cambridge curriculum is dedicated to helping schools develop learners who are confident, responsible, reflective, innovative and engaged. It is designed to give learners the skills to problem solve effectively, apply mathematical knowledge and develop a holistic understanding of the subject.

The *Cambridge Primary Maths* textbooks provide best-in-class support for this problem-solving approach, based on pedagogical practice found in successful schools across the world. The engaging NRICH online resources help develop mathematical thinking and problem-solving skills. To get involved visit www.cie.org.uk/cambridgeprimarymaths

The benefits of being part of *Cambridge Primary Maths* are:
- the opportunity to explore a maths curriculum founded on the values of the University of Cambridge and best practice in schools
- access to an innovative package of online and print resources that can help bring the Cambridge Primary mathematics curriculum to life in the classroom.

This series is arranged to ensure that the curriculum is covered whilst allowing teachers to use a flexible approach. The Scheme of Work for Stage 4 has been followed, though not in the same order and there will be some deviations. The components are:
- Teacher's Resource 4 ISBN: 9781107692947 (printed book and CD-ROM).
- Learner's Book 4 ISBN: 9781107662698 (printed book)
- Games Book 4 ISBN: 9781107685420 (printed book and CD-ROM).

For associated NRICH activities, please visit the *Cambridge Primary Maths* project at www.cie.org.uk/cambridgeprimarymaths

Find the largest number

Maths focus: identifying the value of digits according to their place within a four-digit number.

A game for two or more players

You will need:
- Game cards (page 2).
- A 1–10 spinner (CD-ROM).

How to play

1. Players write their names on the game card.
2. Players take turns to roll the dice. They write the number in **any** box on their game card.
3. Play continues until all boxes on the game card have been filled to make three four-digit numbers.
4. The player with the largest four-digit number scores six points, the next largest five points, and so on.
5. Players add up all the points on their game card. The player with the largest total of points is the winner.

Hexalines

Maths focus: reinforcing the change in place value when a number is multiplied or divided by 10 or 100 and establishing the pattern of multiplying by multiples of 10.

A game for two players

You will need:
- Game board (page 3).
- 15 white counters and 15 black counters (or suitable alternative).
- Two 1–6 dice or 1–6 spinners (CD-ROM).
- A calculator.

How to play

1. Decide who will go first. Player 1 must try to get across the board from left to right (WHITE to WHITE). Player 2 must try to get from top to bottom (BLACK to BLACK).
2. Players take turns to roll both dice. They use the two dice scores to create a number by adding, subtracting, multiplying or dividing the two dice scores together, and then multiplying the answer by 10 or 100 to make a number on the board. Each player can start anywhere on the board.
3. If a player can make one of the numbers on the board, they explain to their opponent how they made it and places one of their counters on that hexagon. Play then passes to the next player. (Calculators can be used to check answers.)
4. If a player cannot make one of the uncovered numbers on the board, the turn passes to their opponent.
5. The winner is the first player to make a continuous line of counters from one side of the board to the opposite side.

Find the largest number – Game cards

Player 1 _____

☐	☐	☐	☐
☐	☐	☐	☐
☐	☐	☐	☐
☐	☐	☐	☐

☐ Score

Player 2 _____

☐	☐	☐	☐
☐	☐	☐	☐
☐	☐	☐	☐
☐	☐	☐	☐

☐ Score

Player 1 _____

☐	☐	☐	☐
☐	☐	☐	☐
☐	☐	☐	☐
☐	☐	☐	☐

☐ Score

Player 2 _____

☐	☐	☐	☐
☐	☐	☐	☐
☐	☐	☐	☐
☐	☐	☐	☐

☐ Score

BLACK

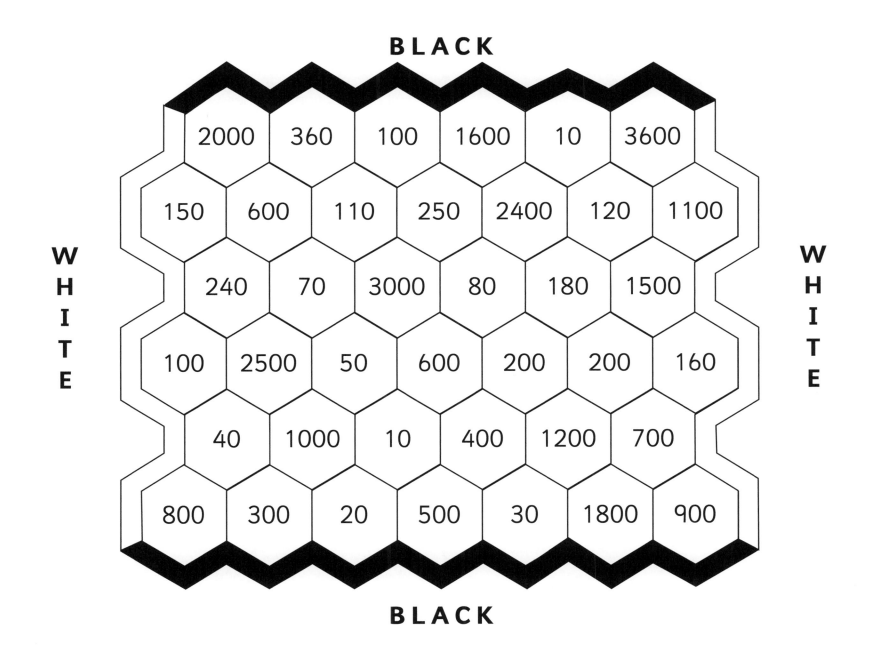

WHITE   **WHITE**

| 2000 | 360 | 100 | 1600 | 10 | 3600 |

| 150 | 600 | 110 | 250 | 2400 | 120 | 1100 |

| 240 | 70 | 3000 | 80 | 180 | 1500 |

| 100 | 2500 | 50 | 600 | 200 | 200 | 160 |

| 40 | 1000 | 10 | 400 | 1200 | 700 |

| 800 | 300 | 20 | 500 | 30 | 1800 | 900 |

BLACK

Hexalines – Games board

Add to 500

Maths focus: choosing an appropriate strategy to add a pair of two-digit numbers.

A game for up to six players

You will need:
- Score chart (page 5).
- A set of dominoes (CD-ROM).
- A pen or pencil.

How to play

1. Spread a set of dominoes face down on the table.
2. Each player starts with 0 points. Players take it in turns to pick a domino and turn it over. They make two different two-digit numbers using the numbers on the domino. For example, the domino below makes the numbers 14 and 41.

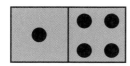

3. Players add their two numbers together and write down the total as the score. For example, 14 + 41 scores 55.
4. If a double domino is revealed, then the two-digit number is doubled.

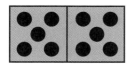

5. Each player keeps a running total of their score using the score card. The first player to reach 500 is the winner.

Difference bingo

Maths focus: choosing an appropriate strategy to subtract a two-digit number from another two-digit number.

A game for a leader and up to six players

You will need:
- Game cards (page 6).
- Game board (page 7).
- 12 counters (or alternative).
- A calculator.
- A pen or pencil and some paper.

How to play

1. Shuffle the Game cards and place them face down.
2. The leader takes two Game cards and shows them.
3. The players calculate the difference between the two numbers. If that difference is on their bingo board they cover the number with a counter.
4. The leader uses a calculator to check the difference between the two numbers and writes down the difference on a piece of paper. The two Game cards are then discarded.
5. The leader takes two further Game cards and players calculate the difference. As before, if the number is on a player's board, they cover it with a counter. Play continues this way until the leader has run out of cards.
6. The winner is the player who has covered the most numbers on their Game board when there are no number cards left.
7. The leader checks the winner's bingo board by comparing the numbers on the board with the numbers on the leader's list.

Add to 500 score chart

Player 1	Player 2	Player 3	Player 4	Player 5	Player 6

Player 1	Player 2	Player 3	Player 4	Player 5	Player 6

Difference bingo – Game cards

56	74	23	15	48	67
92	19	16	94	63	45
83	27	52	76	81	28
31	66	24	38	59	14
42	73	89	91	25	40

1	11	20	47
4	14	29	50
8	15	36	66

1	12	20	49
6	17	25	51
9	19	37	66

3	14	26	44
7	17	29	51
10	21	32	70

4	16	22	44
5	18	25	47
9	21	32	58

2	13	22	50
5	16	24	58
7	19	35	74

3	10	23	45
6	15	24	52
8	18	31	60

Subtract three in a row

Maths focus: subtracting pairs of three-digit numbers.

A game for two players

> **You will need:**
> - Game board (page 9).
> - A set of counters (or alternative) for each player.
> - Paper, pencils and a calculator may be useful.

How to play

1. Players take turns to choose two numbers from the 'Number choices' grid on the game board.
2. They calculate the difference between the two numbers. If that difference appears on the top grid on the game board, they cover it with a counter and have another turn. If the difference is not on the game board, their turn ends and it is the next player's turn.
3. If a player makes a difference that is already covered by a counter, they miss a turn.
4. Players may use a calculator to check their calculations if they disagree on the difference.
5. The first player to place three counters in a row, vertically, horizontally or diagonally, is the winner.

Multiplication five in a row

Maths focus: practising times table facts and reinforcing the meaning of the term 'product'.

A game for two players

> **You will need:**
> - Game board (page 10).
> - Two 1–6 dice.
> - 40 counters (or alternative); 20 of one colour and 20 of a different colour.

How to play

1. Players take turns to roll both dice. They multiply the two dice scores together and place one of their counters on the game board to cover the product of the multiplication.
2. Players can only cover one product each turn. If a player is unable to cover a product on the game board, then they miss that turn.
3. The winner is the first player to cover five numbers in a row – vertically, horizontally or diagonally.

636	130	98	435	329
76	318	285	193	324
294	788	177	864	194
264	807	661	341	8
595	65	24	21	588

Number choices

723	644	109	432	981	625	447	534
699	775	288	511	362	973	529	174
317	240	835	193	876	386	504	219

2	12	18	4	24	16	8	30
10	5	1	15	8	30	15	6
25	8	2	20	3	24	6	5
12	15	6	4	36	18	12	6
18	10	5	9	1	25	20	4
3	2	9	5	30	6	12	12
4	3	16	12	10	8	24	2
18	12	4	16	6	20	24	36

Finding multiples

Maths focus: recognising multiples of 2, 3, 4, 5, 6 and 10 up to the tenth multiple.

A game for two players

You will need:
- Game board (page 12).
- A 1–6 dice.
- Counters (or alternative); two different colours.

How to play
1. Players take it in turns to roll the dice. They then place one of their counters on any number on the board that is a multiple of their dice score.
2. If a player is unable to cover a number on the game board, they miss that turn.
3. The winner is the first player to have four of their counters in a row.

Double dice

Maths focus: practising finding doubles of two-digit numbers.

A game for two players

You will need:
- Game board (page 13).
- Two different coloured 1–6 dice; one to represent the 'tens' digit and one to represent the 'units' digit.
- 20 counters (or alternative); 10 of one colour and 10 of a different colour.

How to play
1. Players take turns to roll both dice to make a two-digit number, for example 36. They then place one of their counters on the number on the board that is **double** their two-digit number. For example, 72 is double 36.
2. The winner is the first player to place three of their counters in a row – vertically, horizontally or diagonally.

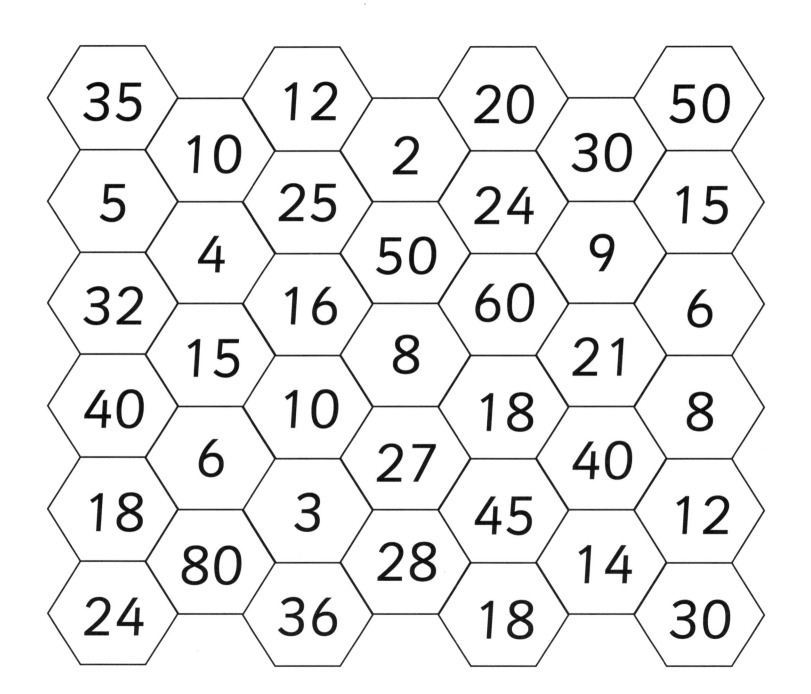

Double dice – Game board

22	24	26	28	30	32
42	44	46	48	50	52
62	64	66	68	70	72
82	84	86	88	90	92
102	104	106	108	110	112
122	124	126	128	130	132

22	24	26	28	30	32
42	44	46	48	50	52
62	64	66	68	70	72
82	84	86	88	90	92
102	104	106	108	110	112
122	124	126	128	130	132

Find the product

Maths focus: practising multiplying a two-digit number by a single-digit number, or 10.

A game for two players

You will need:
- Game board (page 15).
- A calculator.
- Counters (or alternative); two different colours.

How to play

1. Players take turns to choose one number from the circle and one number from the square on the game board. They then multiply the numbers together.
2. If the answer appears on the grid, the player places a counter on the number.
3. The winner is the first player to place four of their counters in a row – vertically, horizontally or diagonally.

Place value

Maths focus: understanding of the value of a digit according to its place value.

A game for two players

You will need:
- Game board (page 16).
- A 1–6 dice.
- A counter (or alternative) for each player.

How to play

1. Players take it in turns to roll the dice. They move forward the number of squares shown on the dice.
2. If the player lands on a square with a number and the score on the dice matches one of the digits in the number, the player moves on as follows:
   - 4 places if it is in the tens column
   - 3 places if it is in the units column
   - 2 places if it is in the tenths column
   - 1 place if it is in the hundredths column.

   If a player lands on a space without a number, play moves immediately to the next player.
3. The first player past the finish is the winner.

   Give less confident players a copy of a place value chart like that shown below.

T	U	●	tenths	hundredths
		●		

135	332	260	204	75	180
316	520	680	250	136	237
272	415	225	156	395	104
50	208	100	166	90	125
830	450	790	158	249	340

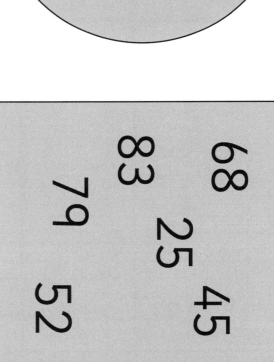

10
2   3
5   4

68   45
83   25
79   52

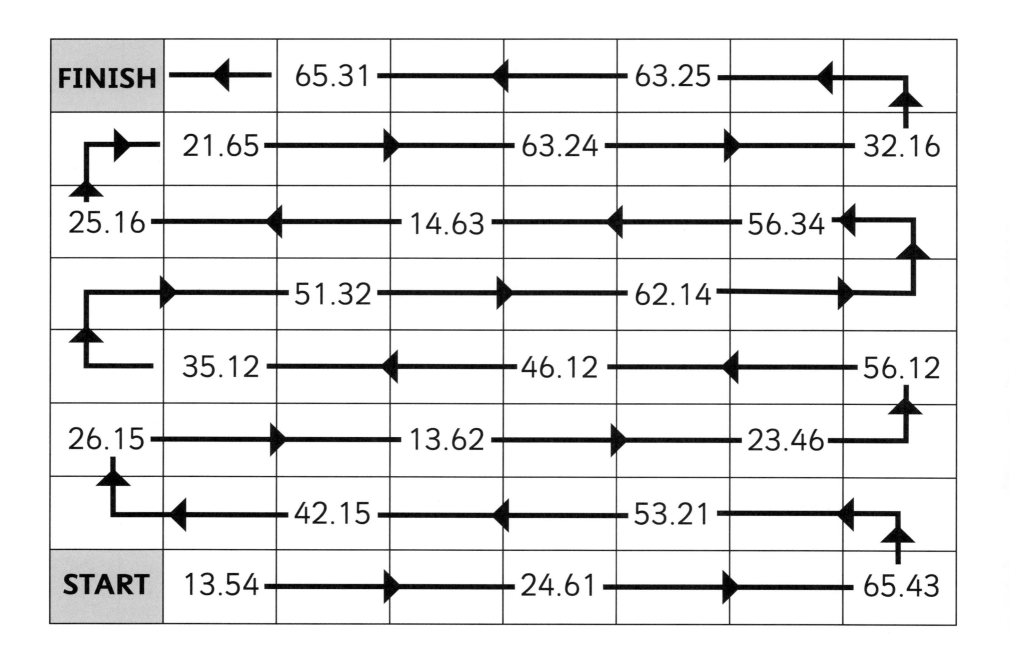

Target number

Maths focus: understanding of the value of a digit according to its place value, and the impact of adding multiples of 1, 10, 100 or 1000.

A game for two players

You will need:
A calculator.

How to play

1. Players agree on a starting number and a target number. For example, start with 3742 and a target of 9653.
2. Players need to reach the target number in four turns by changing one digit at a time. Players take it in turns to suggest one of the digits to change, and challenge the other player to change the number by adding or subtracting a multiple of 1, 10, 100 or 1000.
3. Players must say if they are using addition or subtraction, and then use a calculator to check.
4. For example:
   Turn 1 Player 1: "Change 3742 to 3752."
   Player 2: "Add 10." (check on calculator $3742 + 10 = 3752$)
   Turn 2 Player 2: "Change 3752 to 3652"
   Player 1: "Subtract 100." (check on calculator $3752 - 100 = 3652$)
   Try the following:

Starting number	4941	8729	7491	2275
Target number	3610	5362	3828	7129

Choose your own numbers.

Money dominoes

Maths focus: recognising different ways to represent money amounts in numerals and the written word.

A game for two players

You will need:
Game cards (pages 18–19).
(Alternatively, use the Blank dominoes on the CD-ROM to create your own dominoes that use the local currency.)

How to play

1. Place the game cards face down on the table.
2. Each player chooses seven game cards. The rest are placed in a pile as 'spares'.
3. Players take it in turns to lay a game card on the table. Each turn, a player must place a game card to match one of the end game cards already on the table. If a player is unable to go, he or she takes a game card from the 'spares' pile and tries again. For example:

one dollar and fifty-two cents	$3.50	three dollars and fifty cents	$1.01

4. Play continues in this way until one player has played all of their game cards.

Money dominoes – Game cards

three dollars and fifty cents	$1.01
seven dollars and seven cents	$1.00
fifty cents	$2.08
four cents	$1.25
two dollars and eighty cents	$0.10
seven dollars and two cents	$4.40
one dollar and ten cents	$3.05

one dollar and fifty-two cents	$3.50
one dollar and one cent	$7.07
one dollar	$0.50
two dollars and eight cents	$0.04
one dollar and twenty-five cents	$2.80
ten cents	$7.02
four dollars and forty cents	$1.10

three dollars and five cents	\$0.08	eight cents	\$10.00
ten dollars	\$4.25	four dollars and twenty-five cents	\$0.55
fifty-five cents	\$1.04	one dollar and four cents	\$0.40
forty cents	\$3.55	three dollars and fifty-five cents	\$10.10
ten dollars and ten cents	\$7.70	seven dollars and seventy cents	\$1.40
one dollar and forty cents	\$7.20	seven dollars and twenty cents	\$0.65
sixty-five cents	\$0.05	five cents	\$1.52

Odds and evens

Maths focus: adding numbers and recognising whether the sum is odd or even.

A game for two players

You will need:
- Game board (page 21).
- A set of 0–100 number cards (CD-ROM)
- Two 1–6 dice.
- A counter (or alternative) for each player.

How to play
1. Both players start with their counter on space '1'.
2. Choose which player will be 'odds' and which will be 'evens'.
3. Shuffle the number cards.
4. Turn over one number card at a time. If the number is even then the 'evens' player rolls the two dice and moves forward that number of spaces, if the number is odd then the 'odds' player rolls the dice and moves.
5. Both players can land on the same space.
6. The winner is the first player to reach or pass '64'.

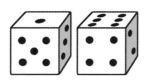

Add to 100

Maths focus: choosing an appropriate strategy to add any pair of two-digit numbers, and quickly deriving pairs of two-digit numbers with a total of 100, e.g. $72 + \square = 100$.

A game for up to four players or teams

You will need:
- A number sentence template for each player/team (page 22).
- A 1–6 dice.

How to play
1. The players/teams take turns to roll the dice.
2. After each roll, the player/team must decide which box in their number sentence to write the score on the die. Players cannot change the position of a number once it is written in a box.
3. The pairs of boxes make two-digit numbers. When deciding where to place the dice score, players should consider that their aim is to make a total that is near to 100.
4. When the players have rolled the dice four times all the boxes are filled and they calculate the total of the two two-digit numbers.
5. The player/team whose total is the closest to 100 is the winner.

Odds and evens – Game board

64	63	62	61	60	59	58	57
49	50	51	52	53	54	55	56
48	47	46	45	44	43	42	41
33	34	35	36	37	38	39	40
32	31	30	29	28	27	26	25
17	18	19	20	21	22	23	24
16	15	14	13	12	11	10	9
1	2	3	4	5	6	7	8

64	63	62	61	60	59	58	57
49	50	51	52	53	54	55	56
48	47	46	45	44	43	42	41
33	34	35	36	37	38	39	40
32	31	30	29	28	27	26	25
17	18	19	20	21	22	23	24
16	15	14	13	12	11	10	9
1	2	3	4	5	6	7	8

Add to 100 – Number sentence templates

Nearest to 500

Maths focus: adding and subtracting pairs of three-digit numbers.

Any number of players

You will need:
- A score card (page 24).
- Three 1–6 dice.
- Pencil and paper for jottings and calculations.

How to play
1. All players start with 500 points. Players must aim to still have 500 points after 10 rounds.
2. Player 1 rolls the three dice. The player makes a three-digit number with the dice scores, then chooses whether to add or subtract the number from his/her current number of points.
3. The player's new total is written on the score card.
4. Play continues in the same way for the other players.
5. The winner is the player whose final total is closest to 500 after 10 rounds.

Divide 4 in a row

Maths focus: deriving division facts for two-digit numbers.

A game for two players

You will need:
- Game board (page 25).
- Two different coloured 1–6 dice.
- Twenty counters (or alternative); ten of one colour and ten of a different colour.

How to play
1. One dice represents the tens digit and the other dice represents the units digit.
2. Players take it in turns to roll the dice to make a two-digit number, for example 36.
3. They then place one of their counters on any number on the board that divides exactly into their two-digit number. For example, 36 can be divided exactly by 2, 3, 4, 6 and 9, which are shown on the board; the player can put their counter on any of these numbers.
4. If a player is unable to go, play passes to the other player.
5. The winner is the first player to place four of their counters in a row – vertically, horizontally or diagonally.

Round	Player 1	Player 2	Player 3	Player 4
1				
2				
3				
4				
5				
6				
7				
8				
9				
Final				

7	8	7	8	4	3	4
6	5	2	3	9	5	8
8	6	5	5	7	9	3
9	4	8	2	4	7	6
6	9	7	3	2	3	9
2	4	9	5	3	5	4
7	8	6	4	2	6	2

7	8	7	8	4	3	4
6	5	2	3	9	5	8
8	6	5	5	7	9	3
9	4	8	2	4	7	6
6	9	7	3	2	3	9
2	4	9	5	3	5	4
7	8	6	4	2	6	2

Divide 4 in a row – Game board

Collect the remainders

Maths focus: practising division with remainders.

A game for two or more players

> **You will need:**
> - Game board (page 27).
> - A 1–6 dice.
> - Coloured counters (or alternative); a different colour for each player.
> - Paper and pencil (for a score sheet).

How to play

1. Players take it in turns to place a counter over a number on the board. They remember the number, then roll the dice and divide their number by the number shown on the dice.
2. Players record any remainder on their score sheet.
3. The winner is the player who has the highest score after all the numbers on the board have been used.

Positive and negative numbers

Maths focus: using negative numbers in the context of changing temperature.

A game for two players

> **You will need:**
> - Game board (page 28).
> - Two 1–6 dice (CD-ROM).
> - One counter (or alternative).

How to play

1. Place the counter at '0' on the board.
2. Each player takes one dice. One player is the 'Sunshine' and one is the 'Snowflake'. Each roll of the dice indicates a change in temperature (in degree Celsius). The value of the change is indicated by the dice score. The direction of change, positive or negative, depends on which player rolled the dice:
   - the 'Sunshine' player moves in a positive direction towards 10°C.
   - the 'Snowflake' player moves in a negative direction, towards −10°C.
3. For example, if the 'Snowflake' player was the first to roll the dice, and they rolled a 4, they would move to −4°C on the board. If the 'Sunshine' player then rolled a 7, they would move 7 spaces along the board towards 10°C, so that they landed on 3°C.
4. Players continue to take turns rolling their die until one player reaches, or passes, their target end of the scale, i.e., 10°C for Sunshine and −10°C for Snowflake. That player is the winner.

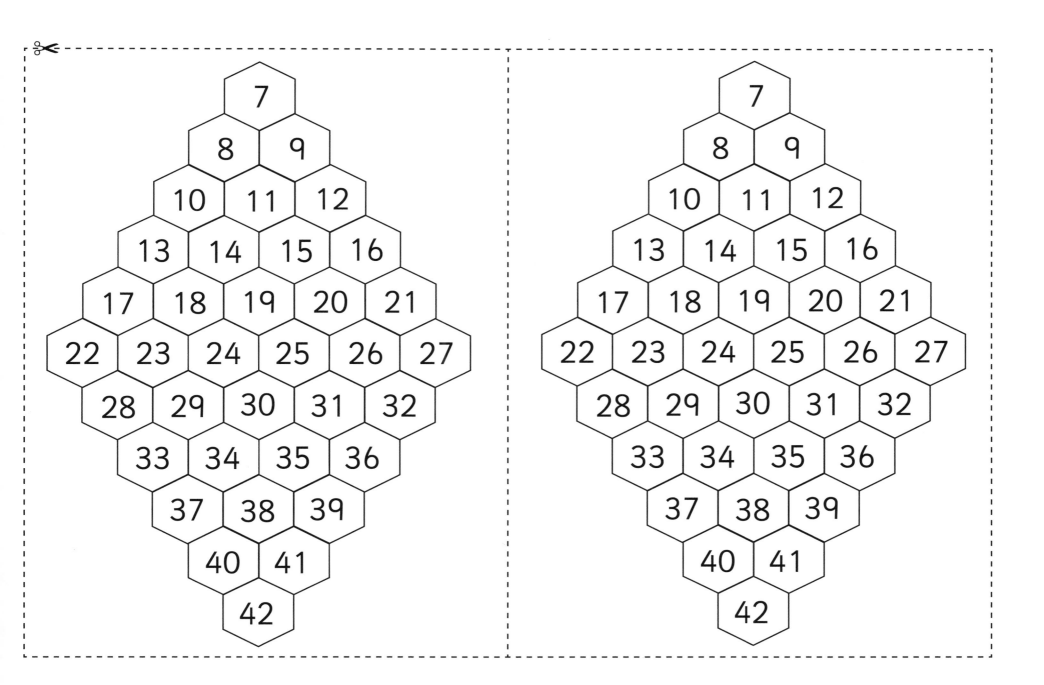

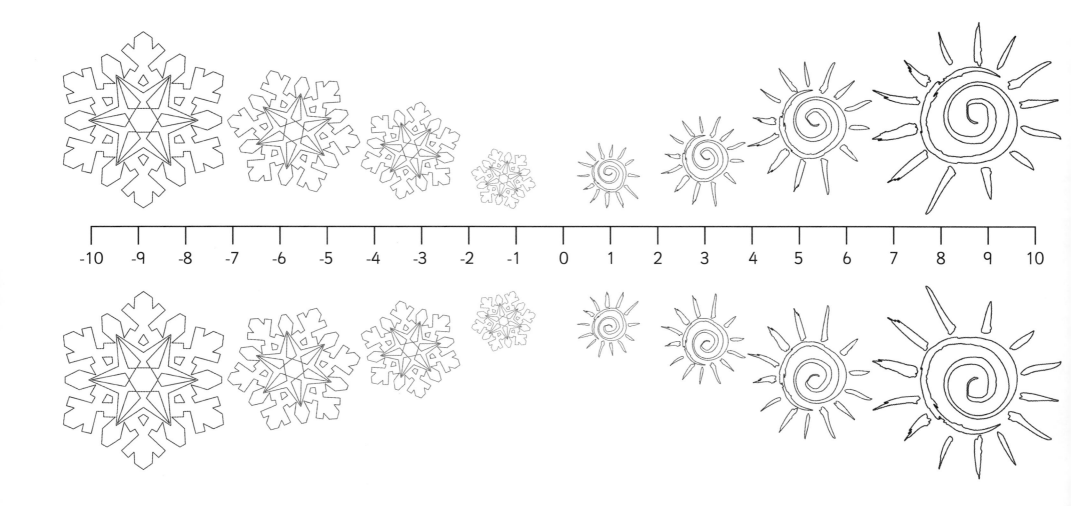

-10 -9 -8 -7 -6 -5 -4 -3 -2 -1 0 1 2 3 4 5 6 7 8 9 10

Positive and negative numbers – Game board

Find a pair

Maths focus: identifying a fraction visually and matching it to the written fraction.

A game for two players

> **You will need:**
> A set of Game cards (pages 30–31).

How to play
1. Shuffle the cards and spread them face down on the table.
2. Players take it in turns to choose two cards.
3. If the cards match, then the player keeps them. If the cards do not match, then the player puts them back in their original position on the table.
4. When all the cards have been picked, the players count their cards.
5. The winner is the player with the most cards.

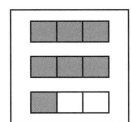

Ratio snap

Maths focus: Recognising equivalent ratios in the context of understanding 'for every' and 'in every'.

A game for two to four players

> **You will need:**
> A set of Game cards (pages 32–37).

How to play
1. Deal all cards to the players.
2. Players place their cards face down in a pile in front of them.
3. Players take it in turns to turn over the top card from their pile and place it face up in a central pile.
4. When a player turns over a card that shows the same ratio as a card on the central pile, all players race to be the first to shout 'SNAP'.
5. The first player to identify an equivalent ratio correctly wins the central pile and adds them to the bottom of their face-down pile.
6. The winner is the player to win all the cards or, alternatively, the player who has the most cards after a pre-determined time.

Example of four cards with equivalent ratios: for every two of one type there is one of another type.

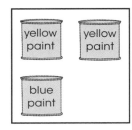 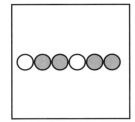  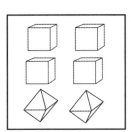

Find a pair – Game cards

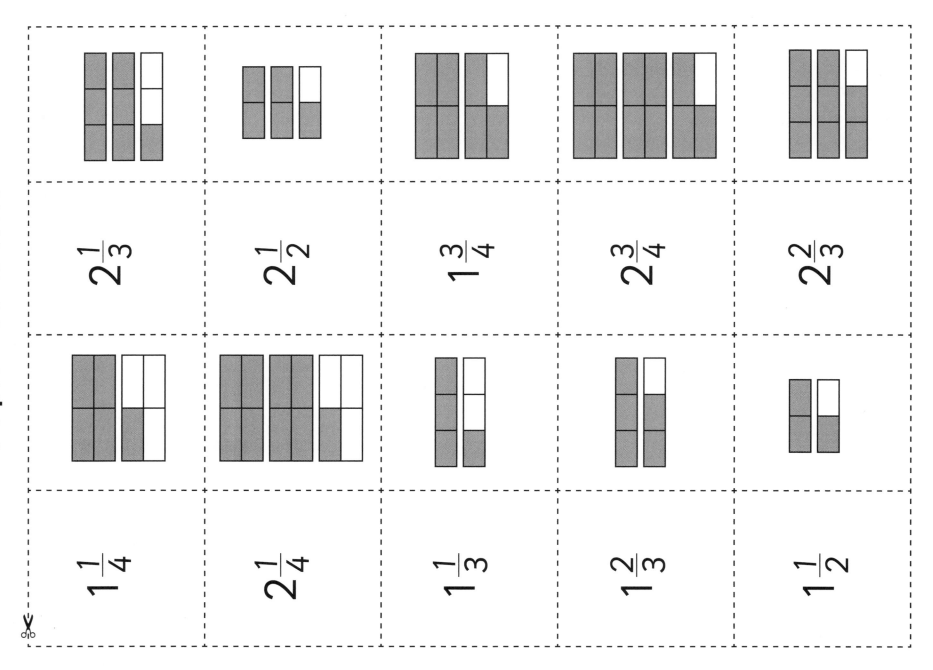

$2\frac{1}{3}$

$2\frac{1}{2}$

$1\frac{3}{4}$

$2\frac{3}{4}$

$2\frac{2}{3}$

$1\frac{1}{4}$

$2\frac{1}{4}$

$1\frac{1}{3}$

$1\frac{2}{3}$

$1\frac{1}{2}$

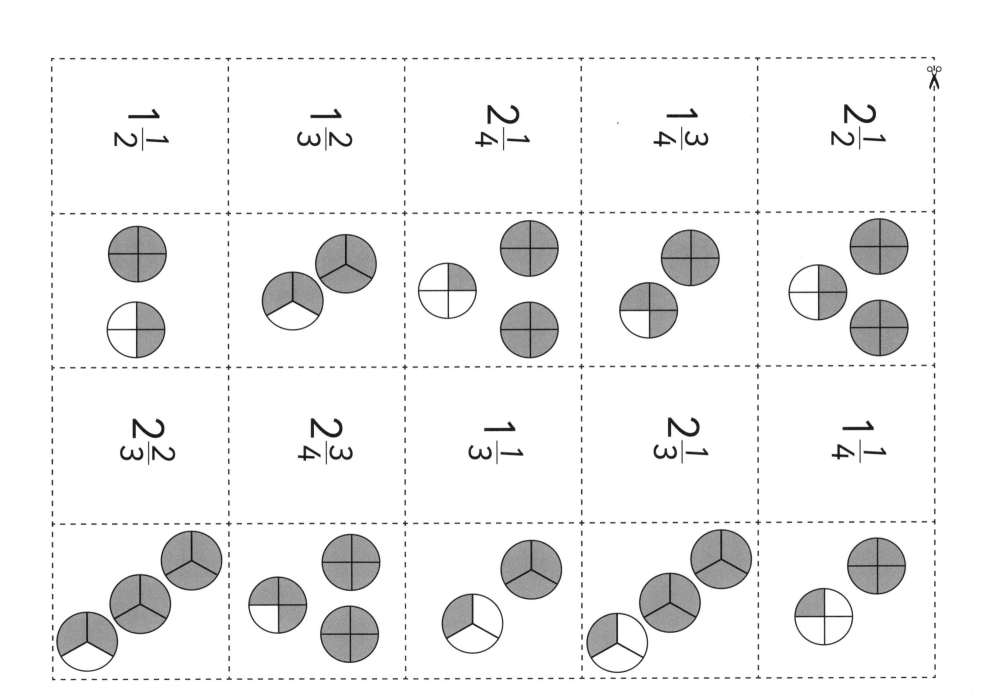

$2\frac{1}{2}$

$1\frac{3}{4}$

$2\frac{1}{4}$

$1\frac{2}{3}$

$1\frac{1}{2}$

$1\frac{1}{4}$

$2\frac{1}{3}$

$1\frac{1}{3}$

$2\frac{3}{4}$

$2\frac{2}{3}$

Ratio snap – Game cards

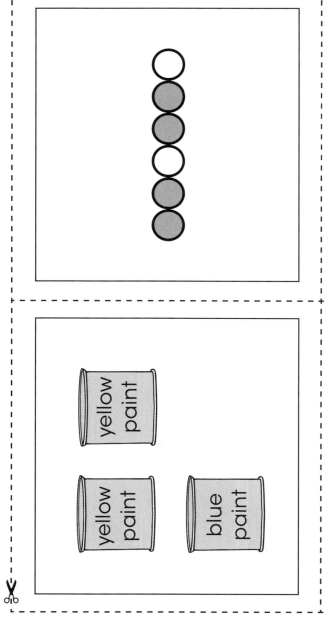

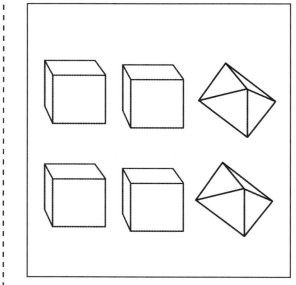

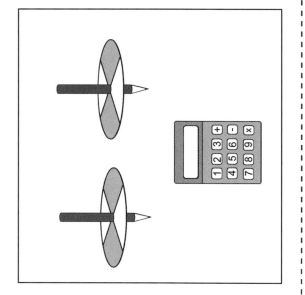

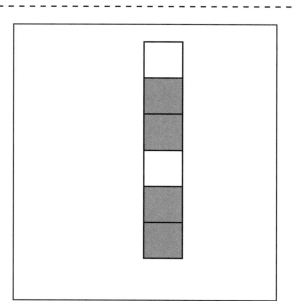

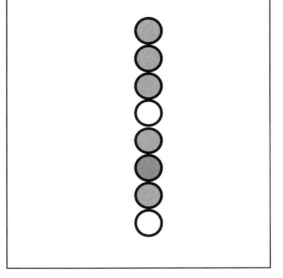

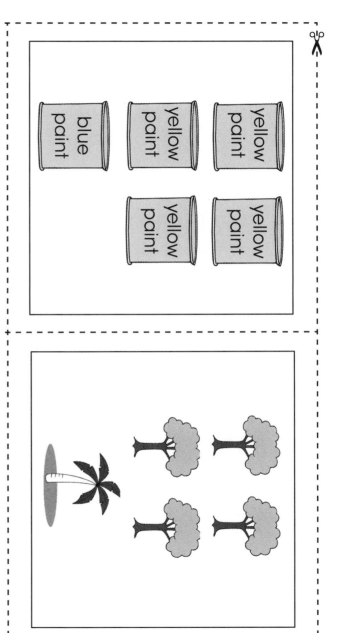

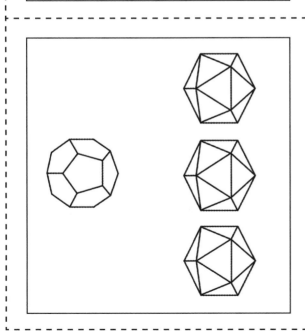

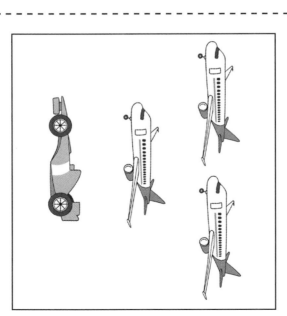

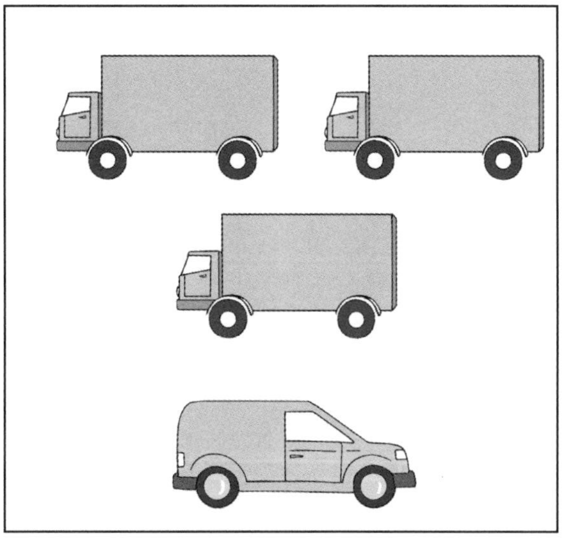

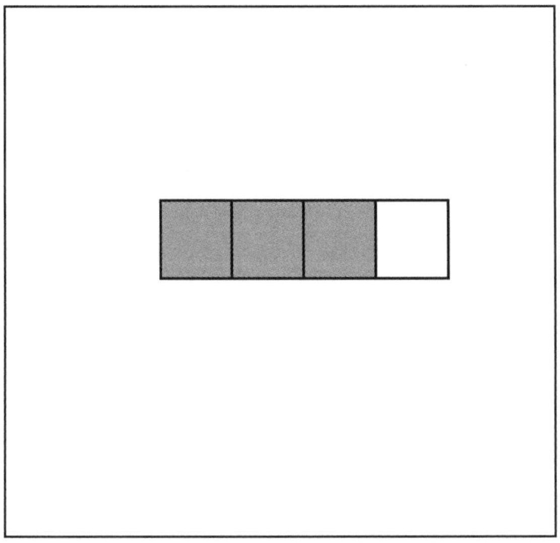

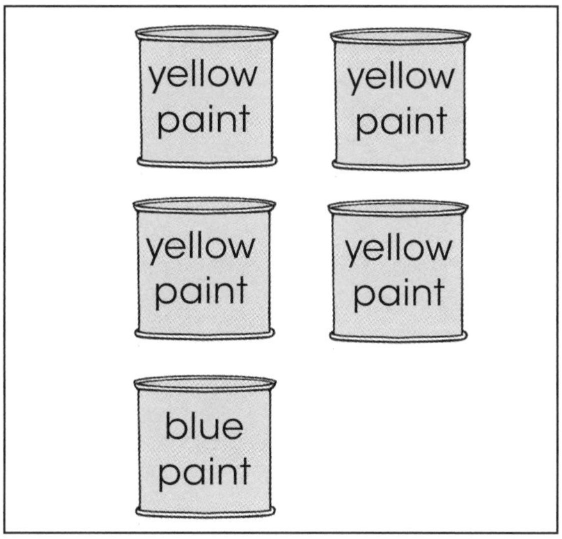
yellow paint
yellow paint
yellow paint
yellow paint
blue paint

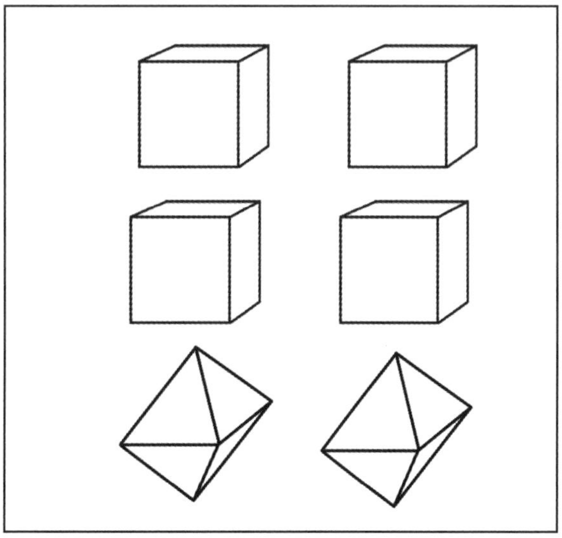

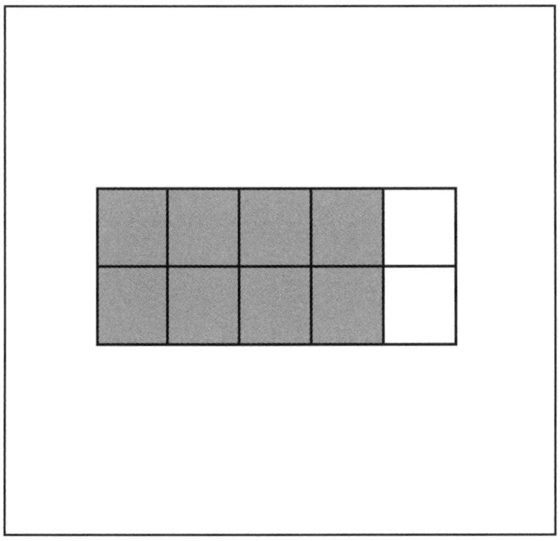

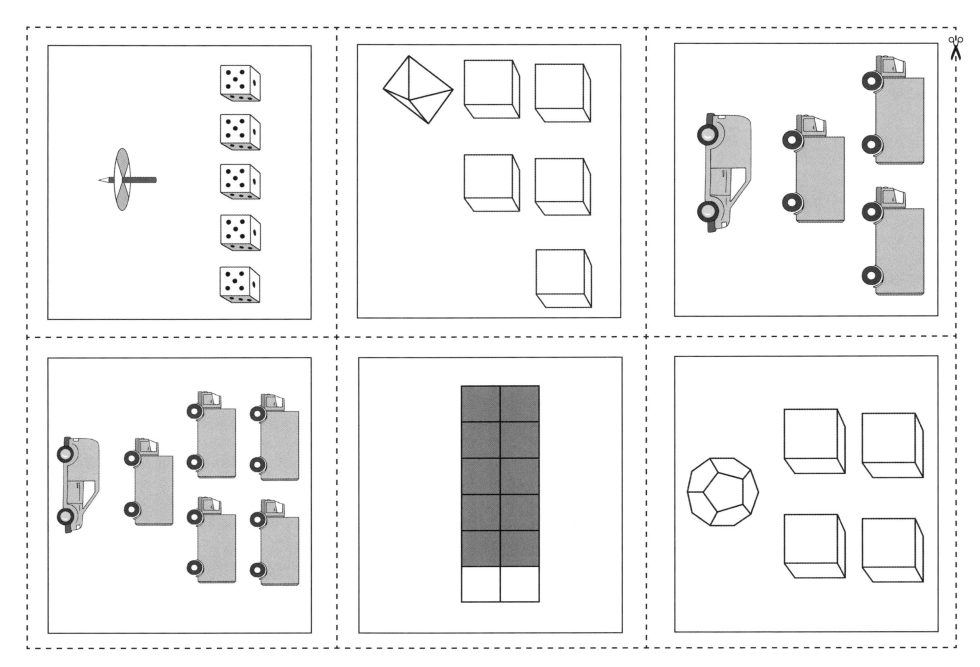

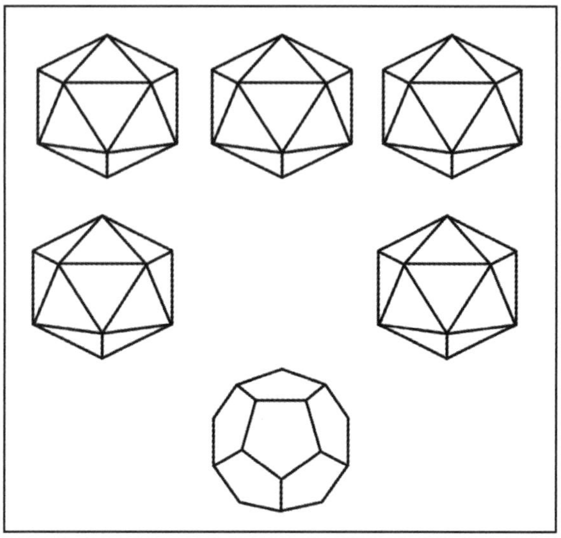

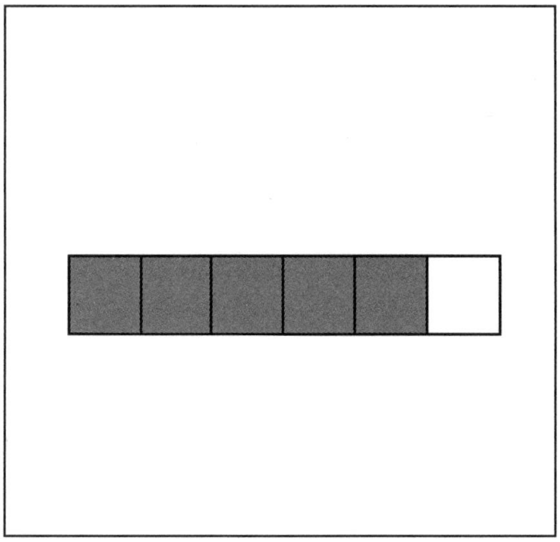

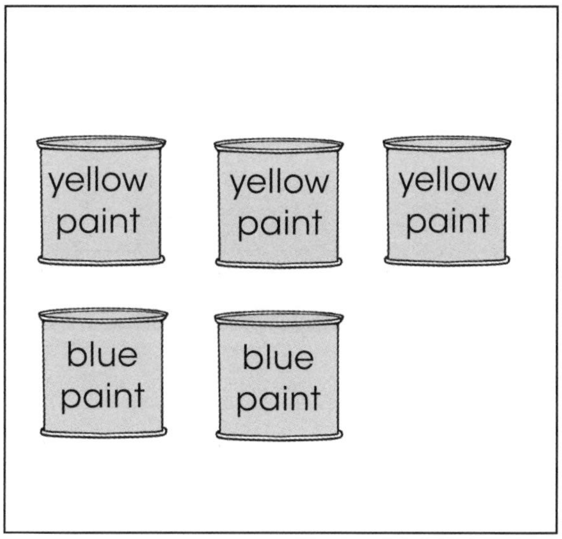
yellow paint
yellow paint
yellow paint
blue paint
blue paint

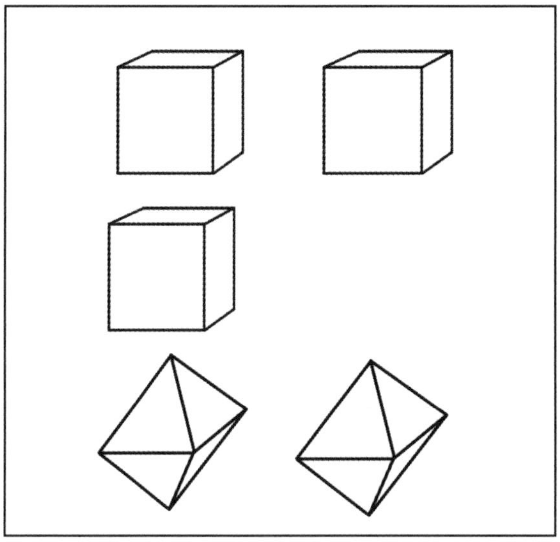

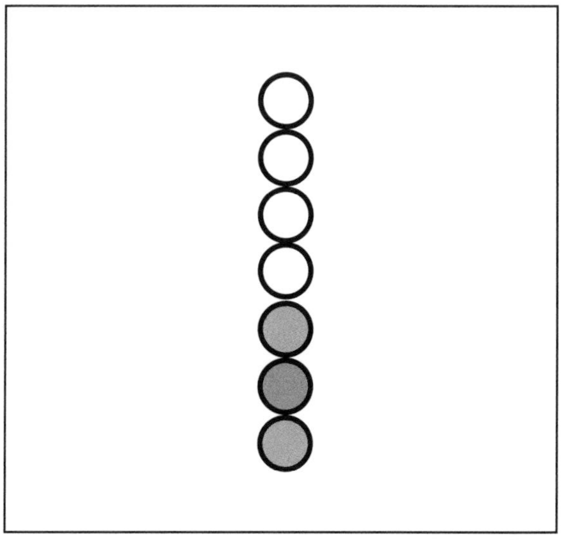

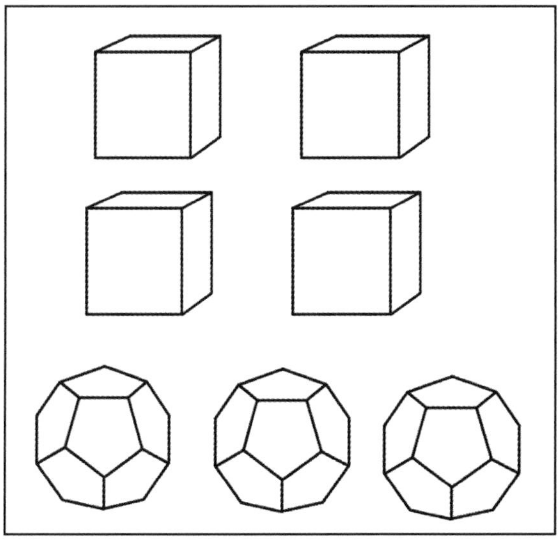

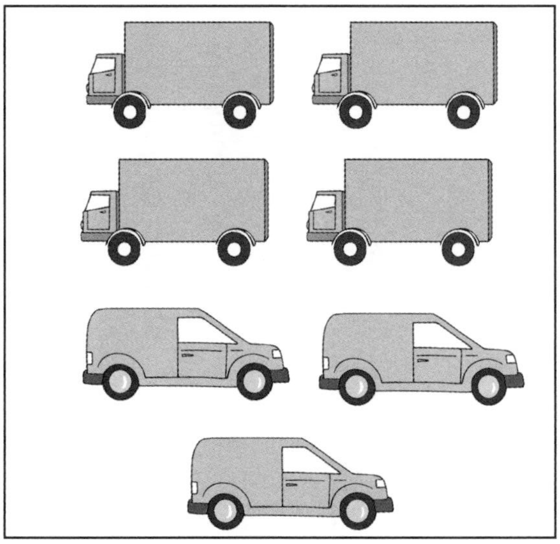

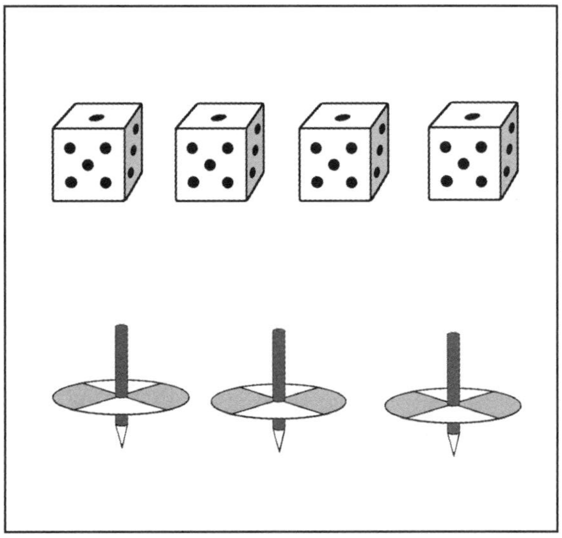

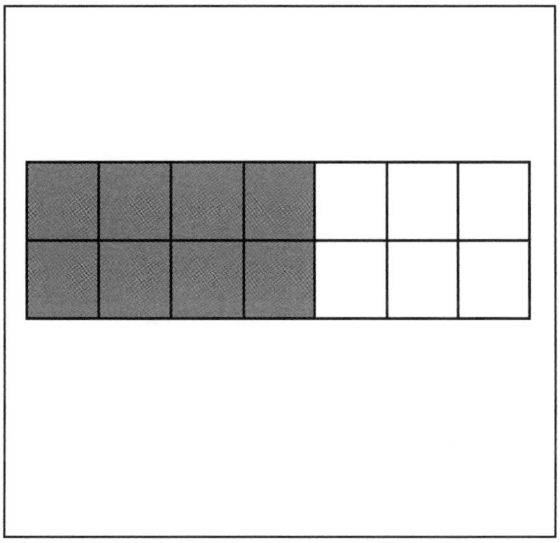

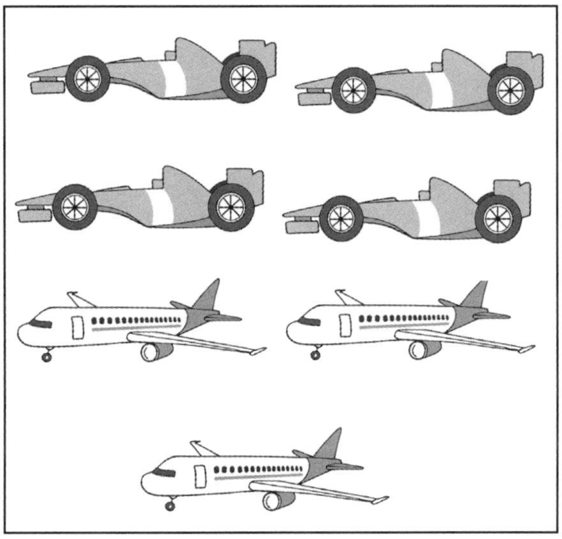

Weighing game

Maths focus: adding weights in grams to get as close as possible to 1 kilogram.

A game for two players

You will need:
- Game cards (page 40).
- Two scales (page 39). Fix an arrow to the centre of each scale with a split pin so that the arrow can be turned to point at any position on the scale.
- Two split pins.

How to play
1. Shuffle the Game cards and place them face down in a pile on the table. Both players start with the arrow on their scales pointing to 0 g.
2. The first player takes a card. They place the card on top of their scale and move the arrow on the scale to the position corresponding to the weight on the card.
3. The second player takes a turn and does the same.
4. Both players take a second card. They add the weight shown on the card to the weight already shown on the scale and move the arrow on their scale to show the new weight.
5. Players must decide whether to keep taking more cards, up to the maximum of five, or to 'stick' at the weight they have, based on how close they are to 1 kg.
6. The player closest to 1 kg is the winner.

'Feeling' a weight is very important for learners to be able to estimate weight. If available, use actual weights in place of the weight cards. Learners have to choose an object they estimate to weigh what the card indicates. If it is a good estimate, then they continue to play. Otherwise the player misses the turn.

Matching time

Maths focus: reading and telling the time to nearest minute on 12-hour digital and analogue clocks.

A game for two to four players

You will need:
Game cards (page 41).

How to play
1. Spread the Game cards, face down, on the table.
2. One turn at a time, each player turns over two cards, but leaves them in their place on the table. If the two cards show the same time, one on an analogue clock, and the other on a digital clock, then the player keeps those cards. If the cards show different times, then they are turned over again and it is the next player's turn.
3. Play continues until all the matching pairs have been found.
4. The winner is the player with the most cards at the end of the game.

Challenge
For a more challenging game, shuffle in the 'Time' cards from the CD-ROM, which include some times that are commonly confused with the times on page 44.

Weighing game – scales

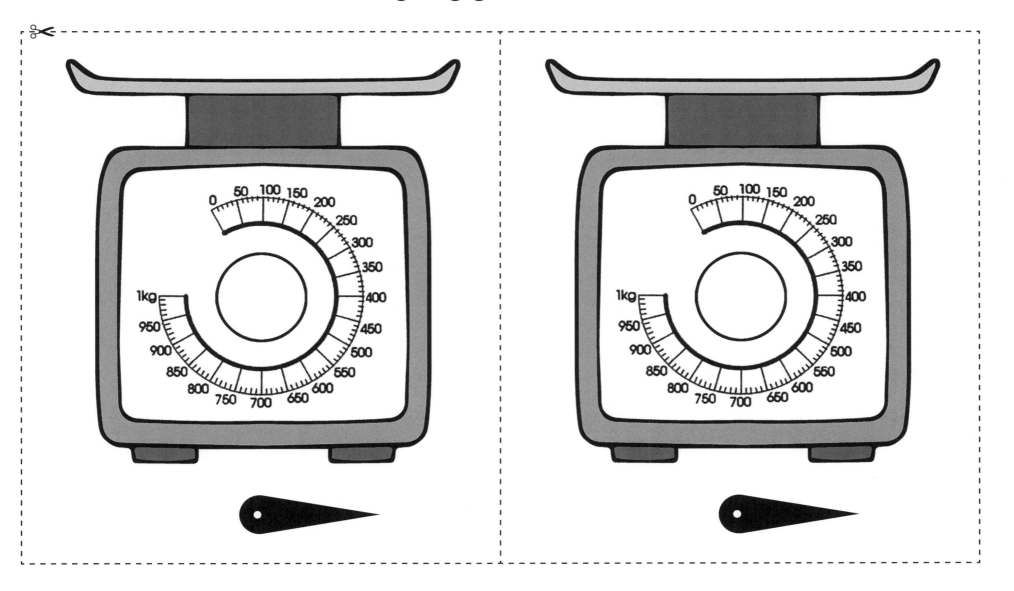

Weighing game – Game cards

50 g	50 g	100 g	100 g	500 g
500 g	200 g	200 g	250 g	250 g
300 g	300 g	350 g	350 g	400 g
400 g	450 g	450 g	0 g	0 g

50 g	50 g	100 g	100 g	500 g
500 g	200 g	200 g	250 g	250 g
300 g	300 g	350 g	350 g	400 g
400 g	450 g	450 g	0 g	0 g

1:28	
4:17	
8:52	
9:33	
12:06	
7:45	

11:21	
2:49	
10:04	
3:11	
5:36	
6:57	

Catch my bus

Maths focus: reading and interpretating data in the form of timetables.

A game for two players

You will need:
- One game card per player (page 42).
- Six counters (or alternatives) per player.

How to play

1. Players place their counters onto six white spaces on their game card without showing the other player.
2. Players take it in turns to say a bus, place and time on the game card. For example: 'Bus 2 at Boxton at 8:45.'
3. If the other player has a counter on that space, then they remove it from their game card.
4. The winner is the player who still has one or more counters on their game card once the other player has lost all of their counters.

Area race game

Maths focus: understanding that area is measured in square units.

A game for two players

You will need:
- Game board (page 43).
- Two different coloured crayons.

How to play

1. Each player has a different coloured crayon.
2. The players take it in turns to colour an area of one, two or three squares in the rectangle on the game board.
3. The player who colours in the last square is the winner.
4. After play has finished, each player records the area of the rectangle that they have coloured in.
5. Play two rounds.

Catch my bus – Game cards

Bus timetable					
	Bus number				
	1	**2**	**3**	**4**	**5**
Amesford	7:15	8:15	10:30	11:30	1:45
Boxton	7:45	8:45	11:00	12:00	2:15
Colebury	8:00	9:00	11:15	12:15	2:30
Danstead	8:22	9:22	11:37	12:37	2:52
Easten	8:51	9:51	12:06	1:06	3:21
Finbridge	9:15	10:15	12:30	1:30	3:45

Bus timetable					
	Bus number				
	1	**2**	**3**	**4**	**5**
Amesford	7:15	8:15	10:30	11:30	1:45
Boxton	7:45	8:45	11:00	12:00	2:15
Colebury	8:00	9:00	11:15	12:15	2:30
Danstead	8:22	9:22	11:37	12:37	2:52
Easten	8:51	9:51	12:06	1:06	3:21
Finbridge	9:15	10:15	12:30	1:30	3:45

Cut along the dashed lines to create two copies of the game board.

Round 1

Player 1_____ square units Player 2 _____ square units

Round 1

Player 1_____ square units Player 2 _____ square units

Round 2

Player 1_____ square units Player 2 _____ square units

Round 2

Player 1_____ square units Player 2 _____ square units

How long is a piece of string?

Maths focus: choosing and using standard metric units and their abbreviations when estimating, measuring and recording length.

A game for two players

You will need:
- Game cards (page 46).
- 1 m of string, thread or wool.
- Scissors.
- A metre stick/rule.
- The string will be cut during the game. If you want to play the game lots of times, then you might like to roll a piece of dough to a length of 1 m and tear pieces off. The dough can then be put back together and rolled again for the next game.

How to play

1. The first player cuts a piece of the string off and discards it. Both players write down on their game card how long they think the (original) piece of string is now.
2. The players measure the string with a metre stick and record the result. The player whose estimate is closest wins one point.
3. Play passes to the second player, who repeats the process described above.
4. Play continues until both players have made three cuts of the string.
5. If, at any time, a player cuts the string so that it becomes less than 10 cm long, the other player wins. Otherwise, the winner is the player with the most points after six rounds.

Making time game

Maths focus: reading and understanding 12 hour digital clock notation.

A game for two players

You will need:
- Game board (page 48)
- A set Game cards (page 47) for each player.

How to play

1. Spread the number cards on the table face down.
2. Shuffle the time cards and place them face down in a pile.
3. Turn the top time card over.
4. The aim is to create a digital time that is as close as possible to the time shown on the time card.
5. Players take it in turns to select a number card and place it into a section on their game board. Once a number has been placed, it cannot be moved.
6. Once a player has placed three cards, they can decide whether or not they wish to take a fourth card.
7. The winner is the player who makes a time on their game board which is the closest to the time on the time card.
8. Players repeat the game five times (so that they have played a total of six games). The player who wins the most rounds is the final winner.

How long is a piece of string? – Game cards

Player 2

Estimate	Actual length	Points

Player 2

Estimate	Actual length	Points

Player 2

Estimate	Actual length	Points

Player 2

Estimate	Actual length	Points

Making time – Game cards

Time cards

1 o'clock	2 o'clock	3 o'clock	4 o'clock
5 o'clock	6 o'clock	7 o'clock	8 o'clock
9 o'clock	10 o'clock	11 o'clock	12 o'clock

Number cards

0	1	2	3	4
5	6	7	8	9
0	1	2	3	4
5	6	7	8	9

Round 1

••

The winner of round 1 was _____

Round 2

••

The winner of round 2 was _____

Round 3

••

The winner of round 3 was _____

Round 4

••

The winner of round 4 was _____

Round 5

••

The winner of round 5 was _____

Round 6

••

The winner of round 6 was _____

Race to the end of the year

Maths focus: reading and using a calendar.

A game for two or more players

> **You will need:**
> * Game board (page 50).
> * A 1–6 dice.
> * A counter (or alternative) for each player.

How to play

1. Players put their counter on the square for 1st October.
2. They take it in turns to throw the dice and move that number of spaces forward on the calendar.
3. If a player lands on a space with an instruction, they follow that instruction before the next player's turn. Players can share spaces.
4. The winner is the first player to reach the square for 31st December.

Challenge

For a more challenging game, change some of the instructions to move between days using two-step instructions such as, 17 Oct – Forward 1 month and 3 days; 8 Nov – Forward 1 month and 2 weeks; 27 Nov – Back 3 weeks and 2 days; 29 Dec – Back 2 months and 4 days.

20 cm perimeter game

Maths focus: drawing quadrilaterals and measuring their perimeters.

A game for two players

> **You will need:**
> * A 1–6 dice (CD-ROM).
> * A ruler.

How to play

1. Each player throws the dice three times. Each number thrown gives the player the length of one side of a quadrilateral in centimetres.
2. The player constructs a quadrilateral using the three lengths given on the dice, completing the shape by joining the remaining two corners together with a straight line.
3. The player measures the last side of the quadrilateral and adds it to the total of the three other sides to find the perimeter.
4. The player whose quadrilateral has a perimeter closest to 20 cm is the winner.

October

M	T	W	T	F	S	S
	1 START	2 Back 3 days	3	4 Forward 1 week	5	6
7	8	9	10	11	12	13
14	15 Go to 8th November	16	17	18	19 Back 1 week	20
21 Forward 2 weeks	22	23	24	25	26	27 Forward 1 month
28	29	30	31 Forward 4 days			

November

M	T	W	T	F	S	S
				1	2 Forward 1 month	3
4	5 Forward to Friday	6	7	8	9	10
11	12	13 Go to 29th October	14	15	16 Back to Sunday	17
18	19	20	21 Back 2 weeks	22	23	24
25 Forward 1 week	26	27	28	29	30 Go to 5th December	

December

M	T	W	T	F	S	S
						1 Back to Wednesday
2	3	4 Back 2 weeks	5	6	7	8
9 Forward 1 week	10	11	12	13	14	15 Back 1 week
16	17	18	19 Forward to Sunday	20	21 Go to 10th December	22
23	24 Back 2 weeks	25	26	27 Back 1 month	28	29
30	31 FINISH					

Race to the end of the year – Game board

How much water?

Maths focus: choosing and using standard metric units and their abbreviations when estimating, measuring and recording capacity.

A game for two players

You will need:
- A 1 litre measuring cylinder.
- A jug with 1 litre of water.
- A tray to catch spills.

How to play

1. Player 1 pours away some water from the jug that contains 1 litre of water. Both players write down how much water they think is in the jug now.
2. The players measure the amount of water by pouring it into a measuring cylinder. The player whose estimate is closest to the actual amount of water in the jug wins one point.
3. Pour the water from the measuring cylinder back into the jug, ready for player 2 to take a turn.
4. Play continues until both players have poured away three amounts of water.
5. If, at any time, a player pours away water so that the amount in the jug becomes less than 100 ml, the other player wins. Otherwise, the winner is the player with the most points at the end of six rounds.

Speedy modelling game

Maths focus: choosing units of time to measure time intervals.

A game for two teams

You will need:
- A record sheet per team (page 53).
- Game cards (page 54); the blank cards enable more objects to be added to the list if desired.
- Modelling clay/dough, toy building bricks or interlocking cubes.
- Stopwatches.

How to play
1. Shuffle the game cards and place them face down on the table.
2. One player from the first team takes a card and does not show it to anybody else.
3. A player from the other team with the stopwatch presses the start button and the player begins to make a model of the object written on the card using the bricks or cubes.
4. The player's team tries to guess which object is being modelled. Once they guess correctly, the stopwatch is stopped and the time for that team is recorded on their record sheet.
5. The second team takes a turn.
6. Play continues until all players have made a model.
7. The times for each team are added up. The team with the fastest total time wins.

Please note, that if players struggle making the words on the cards using modelling clay, ask them to draw the object instead.

Rectangle race

Maths focus: constructing rectangles of a given area and perimeter using 1 cm squares.

A game for two players

You will need:
- Player pieces (page 55). It might be helpful to use different coloured paper for player 1 and player 2.
- Game cards (page 56).

How to play
1. Each player has a set of player pieces. Inform the player that each square in their playing pieces represents a 1 cm^2 square (please note that for ease of use, the squares are not actually 1 cm^2). The game cards are shuffled and placed face down on the table.
2. Turn over one game card.
3. The players race to make some of their pieces into a rectangle with the properties shown on the card.
4. The player who completes their rectangle first wins.
5. Play more rounds, or play the game in teams.

Speedy modelling game – Record sheets

Team 1

Times	Time total

Team 2

Times	Time total

Speedy modelling game – Game cards

house	tree	square	cup	flower
fish	chair	bear	bed	rectangle
glasses	elephant	table	flag	bag

car	sphere	pyramid	shoe	pencil
snail	book	frame	cuboid	circle
t-shirt	hand	person	cone	semi-circle

Rectangle race – Player pieces

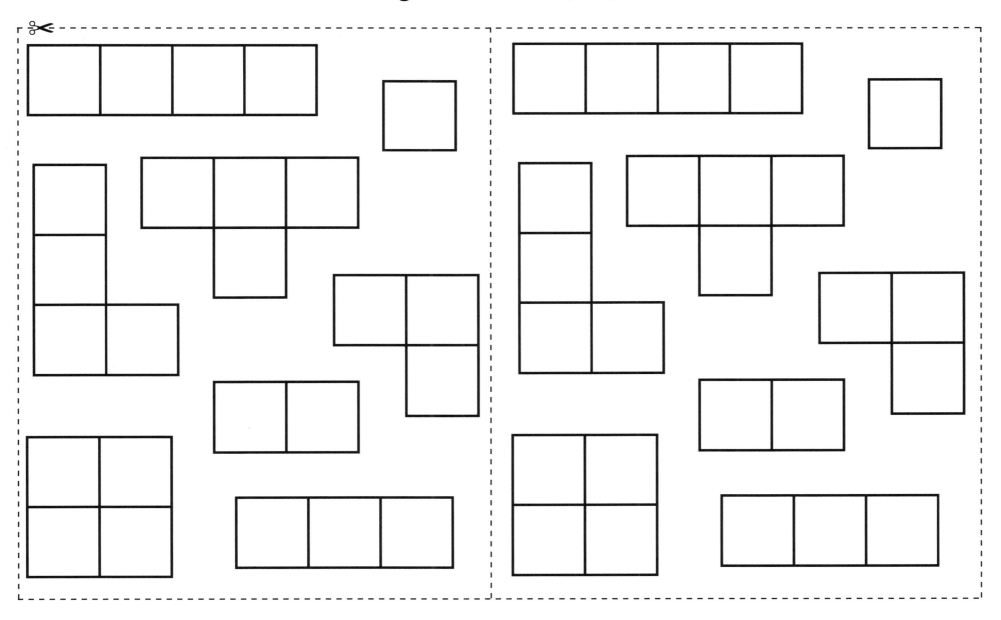

Rectangle race – Game cards

area 15 cm² perimeter 16 cm	area 9 cm² perimeter 12 cm
area 24 cm² perimeter 20 cm	area 8 cm² perimeter 12 cm
area 20 cm² perimeter 18 cm	area 12 cm² perimeter 14 cm
area 12 cm² perimeter 16 cm	area 16 cm² perimeter 16 cm

area 15 cm² perimeter 16 cm	area 9 cm² perimeter 12 cm
area 24 cm² perimeter 20 cm	area 8 cm² perimeter 12 cm
area 20 cm² perimeter 18 cm	area 12 cm² perimeter 14 cm
area 12 cm² perimeter 16 cm	area 16 cm² perimeter 16 cm

Pick up 25 sticks

Maths focus: understanding of the convention behind how tally marks are used.

A game for two to four players

You will need:
- Game board (page 58).
- Game cards (pages 59–60).
- A counter (or alternative)for each player.
- A 1–6 dice.

How to play

1. Starting from 'Start' on the game board, the players take it in turns to throw the dice and move forward that number of places on the board.
2. On some squares there is a choice of direction to follow. The player collects the number of 'sticks' indicated on the square they land on by taking that number of 'I' cards.
3. If a player collects a set of 5 'sticks', then they are exchanged for a 'IIII' card.
4. If a player lands on a 'drop' square, they put that number of sticks back. (The player may have to swap a 'IIII' card for 5 'sticks' to be able to put back the correct number of 'sticks'.)
5. The winner is the player who finishes the game with the total nearest to 25.

Pictogram game

Maths focus: collecting, organising, presenting and interpreting data in a pictogram.

A game for up to five players

You will need:
- Game board (page 61).
- Game cards (page 62).
- Two 1–6 dice or two 1–6 spinners (CD-ROM).
- Small objects to represent seeds, e.g. beads or pebbles.

How to play

1. The first player rolls both dice and calculates the difference between the two dice scores. They take that number of 'seeds'. For example, if Player 1 rolls a 6 and 4, the difference is 2 and they take 2 seeds. Play then passes to the next player.
2. Each time a player has five 'seeds' they can exchange them for a plant pot card and place it on the pictogram.
3. The game ends when all the whole plant pot game cards have been placed on the pictogram, or one player has collected more than 35 seeds.
4. Players swap any remaining seeds for part of a plant pot by folding or cutting along the appropriate line on a plant pot card that is divided into 5 sections, the bottom section only for 1 seed, the bottom two sections for 2 seeds etc. They place this part on the pictogram.
5. The players record their totals. The winner is the player with the greatest total.

START →	3	2	4	1 →	4	2	drop 1
				↓ 1			↓ 1
2	2	1	4 ←	drop 3 ←	2	3	1
↓ drop 2					↓ 2		
3 →	3	1	2 →	4	3 →	drop 4	1
			↓ 4				↓ 4
END	1	drop 10 ←	1	4	drop 5	2 ←	1

Pick up sticks – Game cards

Pictogram of seeds collected

Number of seeds	Player 1	Player 2	Player 3	Player 4	Player 5
35					
30					
25					
20					
15					
10					
5					
0					
Total number of seeds					

Pictogram game - Game cards

Carroll diagram game

Maths focus: use Carroll diagrams to sort data and objects using two or three criteria.

A game for two or four players

You will need:
- Game board (page 64).
- Game cards (page 65).

How to play
1. Each player selects one section of the game board (or two sections if there are two players).
2. Spread the game cards face down on the table.
3. The first player begins by turning over a card. If the number sentence belongs in their section of the Carroll diagram they place it there, otherwise it is returned to the table, face down. Play passes to the next player.
4. The first player to fill their section of the game board with four number sentences is the winner.

Sporting bar graph game

Maths focus: interpret data in bar charts (intervals labelled in twos, fives, tens or twenties).

A game for two players

You will need:
Game cards (pages 66–69).

How to play
1. Shuffle the cards and give each player seven cards, face down.
2. The first player looks at their top card and chooses a sport. The other player looks at their top card.
3. The players compare the score of the chosen sport. The player with the highest score wins both the cards and places them at the bottom of their pile. Play passes to the second player.
4. The game ends when one player has all of the cards. That player is the winner.

	> 50	not > 50
multiple of 10		
not a multiple of 10		

Carroll diagram – Game board

Carroll diagram number sentence – Game cards

$48 + 12$	5×4	$107 - 9$	3×4
$30 - 22$	$100 - 20$	$\frac{1}{4}$ of 40	$35 + 30$
$\frac{1}{2}$ of 150	$13 + 29$	double 35	$60 - 20$
double 15	9×9	$32 \div 4$	$\frac{1}{2}$ of 200

Sporting bar graph – Game cards

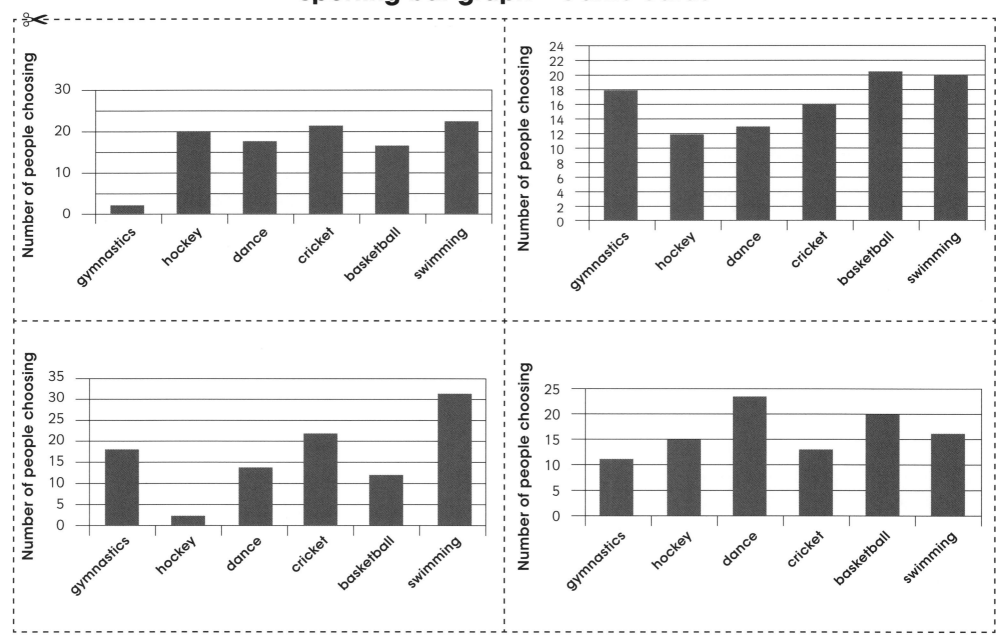

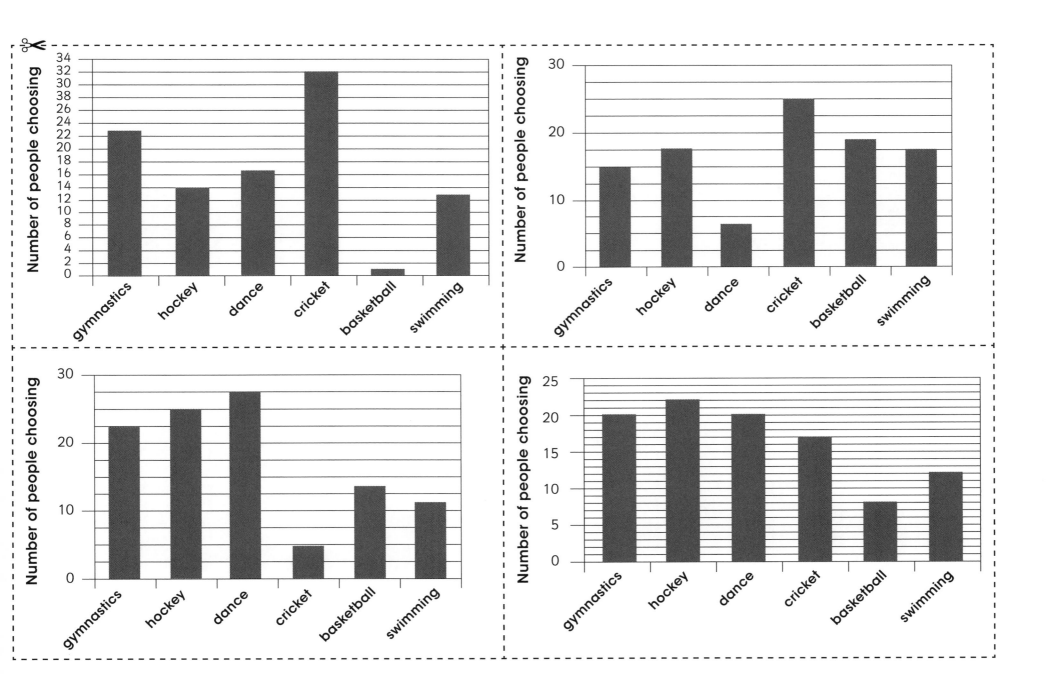

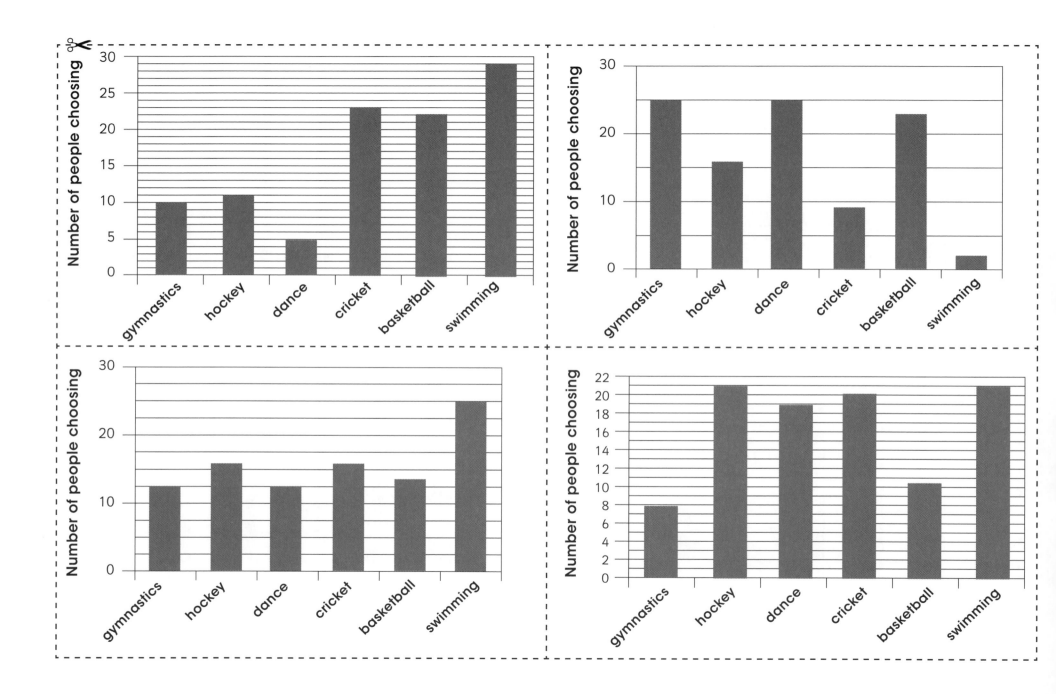

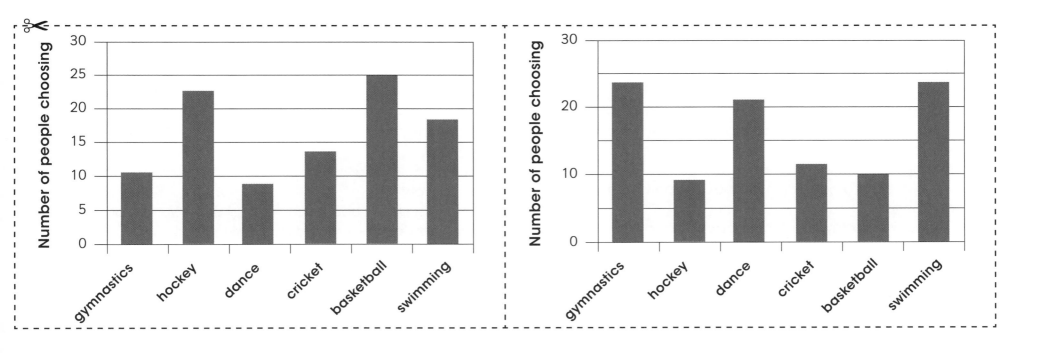

Tree diagram game

Maths focus: using a tree diagram to sort numbers according to their properties.

A game for two or three players

You will need:
- Game board (page 71).
- A set of numbers from the grid below.

How to play
1. One player spreads the numbers face up on the table.
2. Players take it in turns to select a number and place it in the correct box on the tree diagram.
3. If there is already a number in the box, the new number is placed on top.
4. The winner is the player who correctly places a number in the last empty box.

10	11	12	13	14	15	16	17
18	19	20	21	22	23	24	25
26	27	28	29	30	31	32	33

Venn diagram game

Maths focus: use Venn diagrams to sort data and objects using two or three criteria.

A game for two players

You will need:
- Game board (page 72).
- 16 counters (or alternative); eight each of two different colours.
- Two 1–6 dice or 1–6 spinners (CD-ROM).

How to play
1. The first player throws both dice and multiplies the two dice scores together.
2. The player puts a counter in the part of the Venn diagram where their product should go.
3. The second player takes their turn.
4. As the game continues, counters can only be placed in sections of the Venn diagram where that player does not already have a counter.
5. The game ends when one player has a counter in every section of the Venn diagram. That player is the winner.

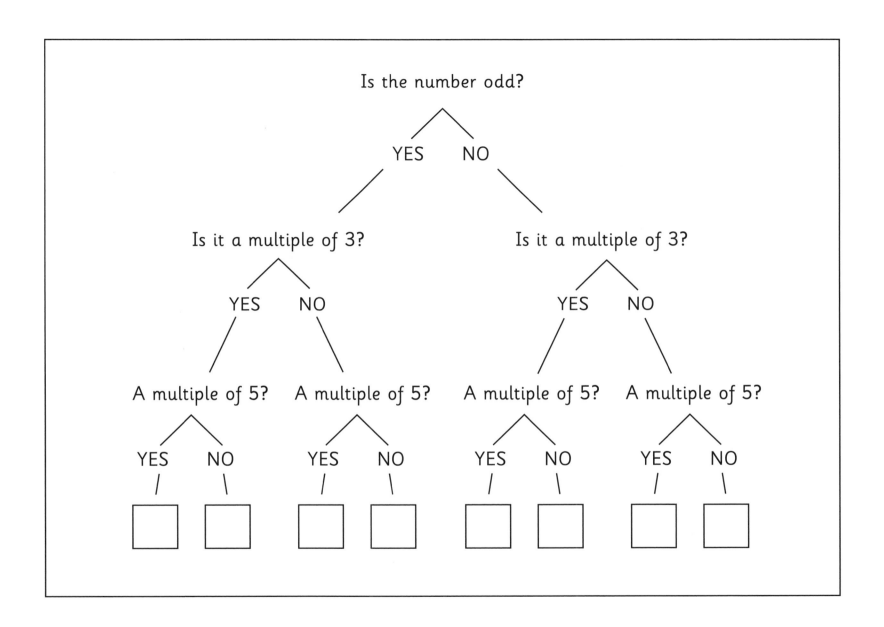

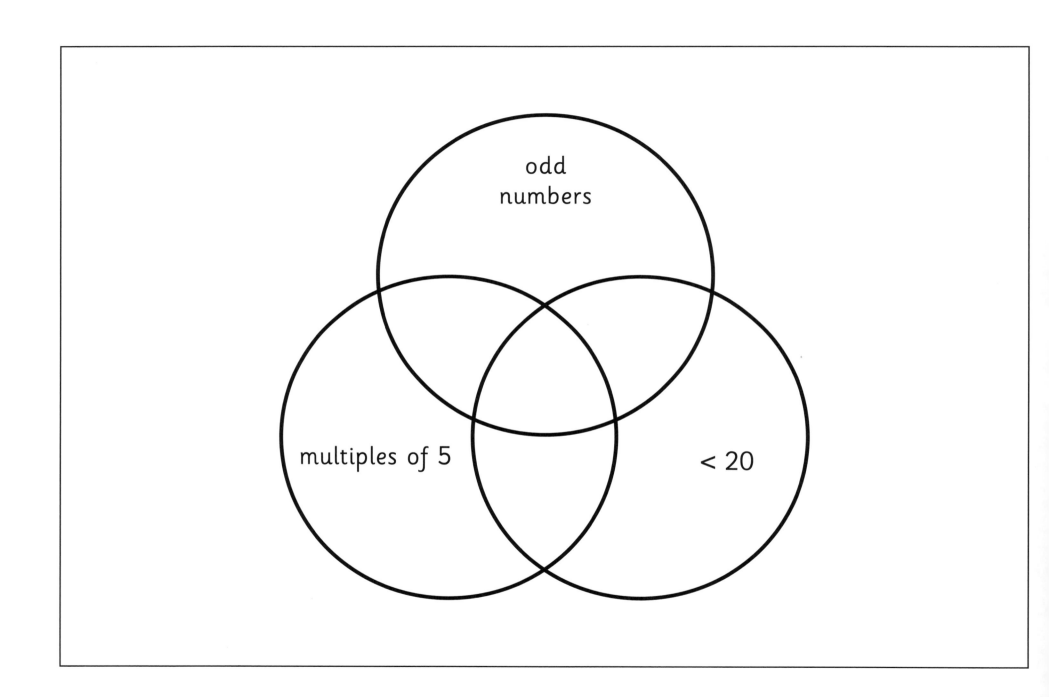

Identifying right angles

Maths focus: describing and identifying the position of a square on a grid of squares where rows and columns are numbered and/or lettered.

A game for two players

You will need:
- Game board (page 73).
- Two different coloured 1–6 dice or 1–6 spinners (CD-ROM).
- Paper and pencil (for recording scores).

How to play
1. One dice represents the first number of an ordered pair. The second dice represents the second number of an ordered pair. Player 1 rolls both dice to get an ordered pair and finds the corresponding shape on the game board. For example, if the dice scores are 1 and 6, the player finds the shape at (1, 6), a triangle.
2. Player 1 counts the number of right angles in the shape, this is their score.
3. Player 2 takes a turn and play continues.
4. Both players keep a running total of their scores. The winner is the first player to get 15 points.

Shape bingo

Maths focus: pairing name with respective shape.

A game for up to 18 players

You will need:
- Game cards (page 74).
- Game board (pages 75–79) for each player.
- Counters (or alternative).

How to play
1. Decide who will be the caller; either the teacher or another adult.
2. The caller shuffles the cards then calls out the shape that is written on each card, one at a time.
3. Players who have the shape on their game board cover it with a counter. (Please note that the game boards should be 3×3 grids.)
4. The first player to cover all their shapes shouts 'Bingo' and is the winner.

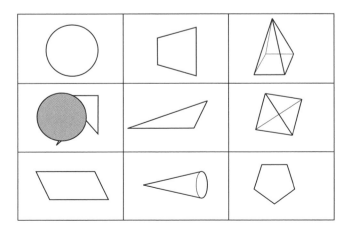

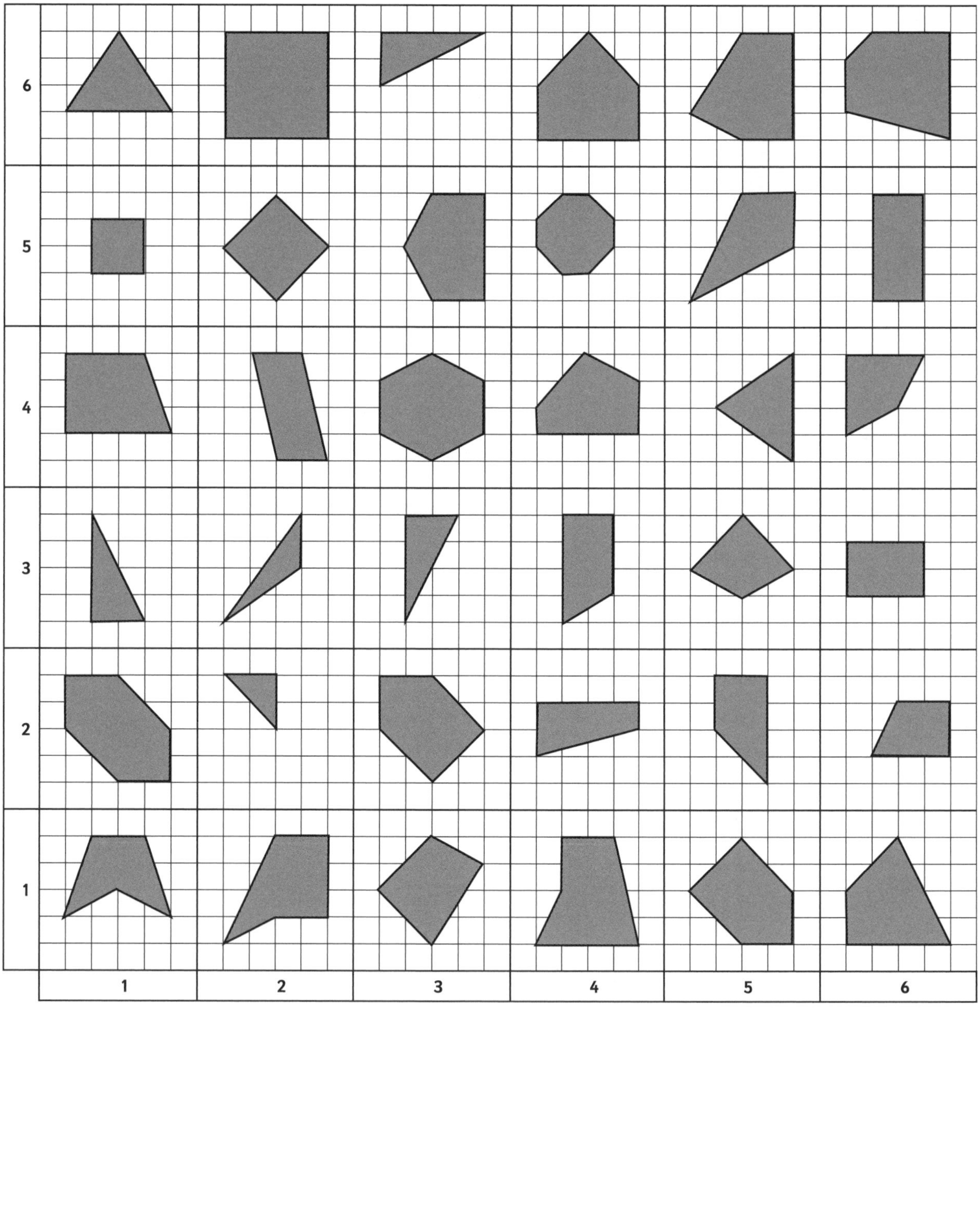
6
5
4
3
2
1
1
2
3
4
5
6

isosceles triangle	equilateral triangle	regular pentagon
regular hexagon	regular octagon	irregular pentagon
irregular hexagon	irregular octagon	circle
right-angled triangle	cube	cuboid
semi-circle	irregular quadrilateral	parallelogram
rectangle	square	cone
square-based pyramid	tetrahedron	cylinder
triangular prism	hexagonal prism	scalene triangle

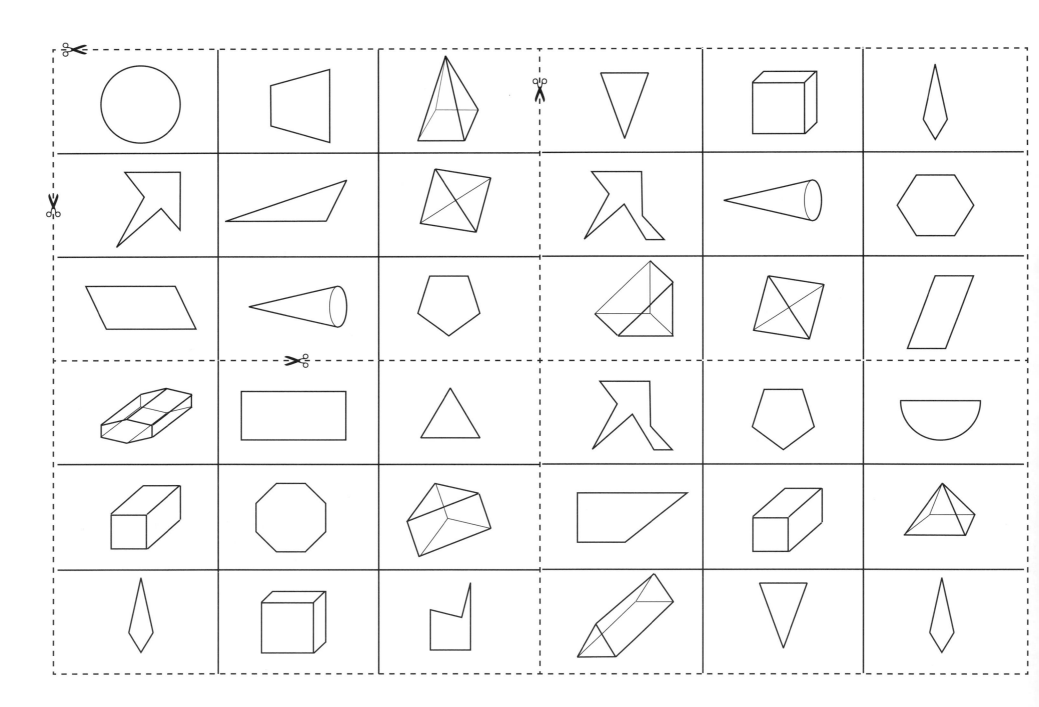

Shape bingo – Game boards

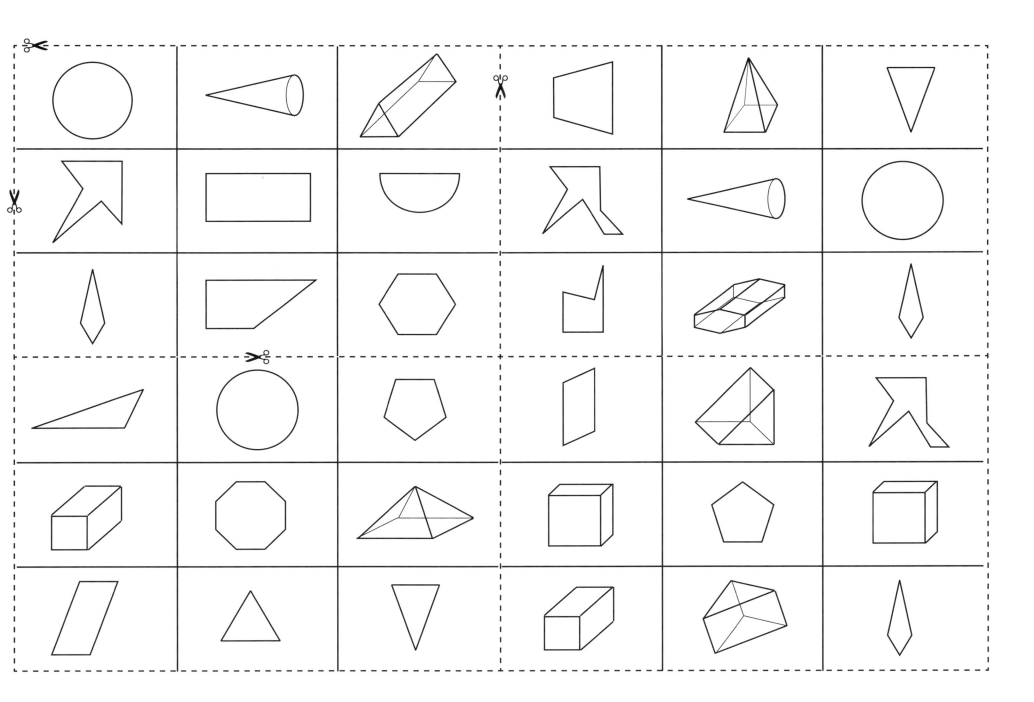

Shape bingo – Game boards

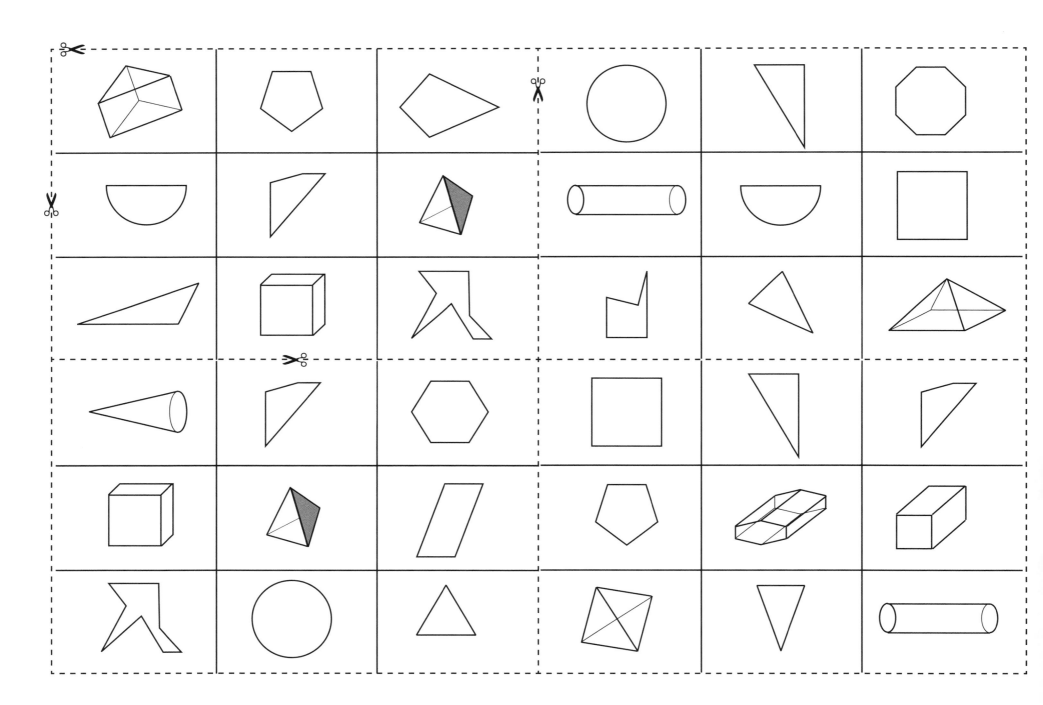

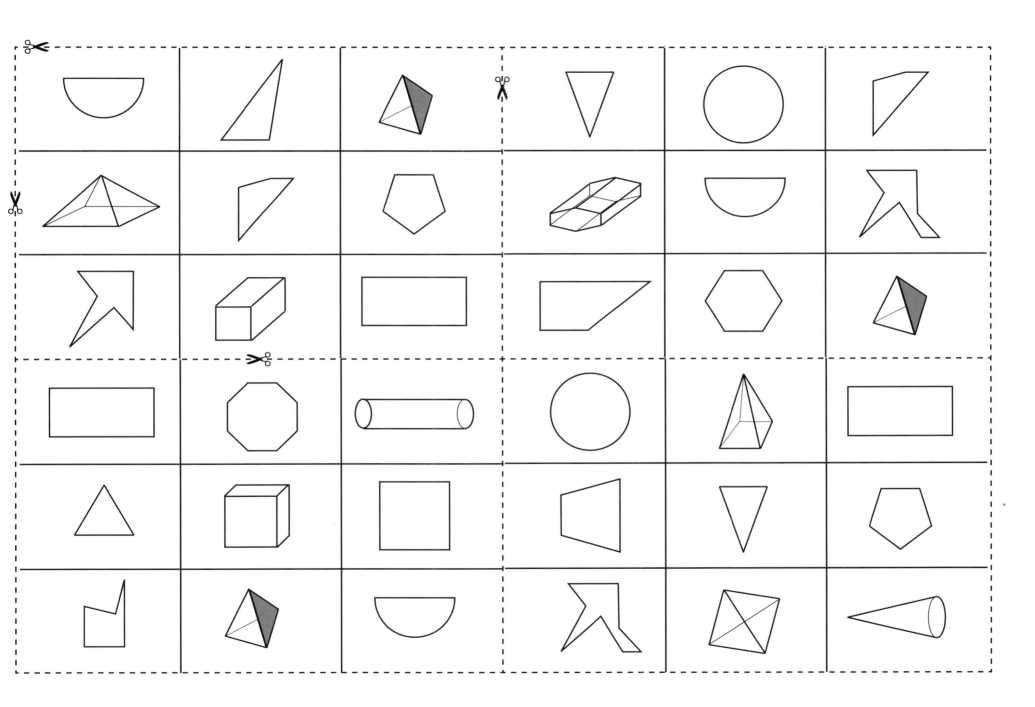

Shape bingo – Game boards

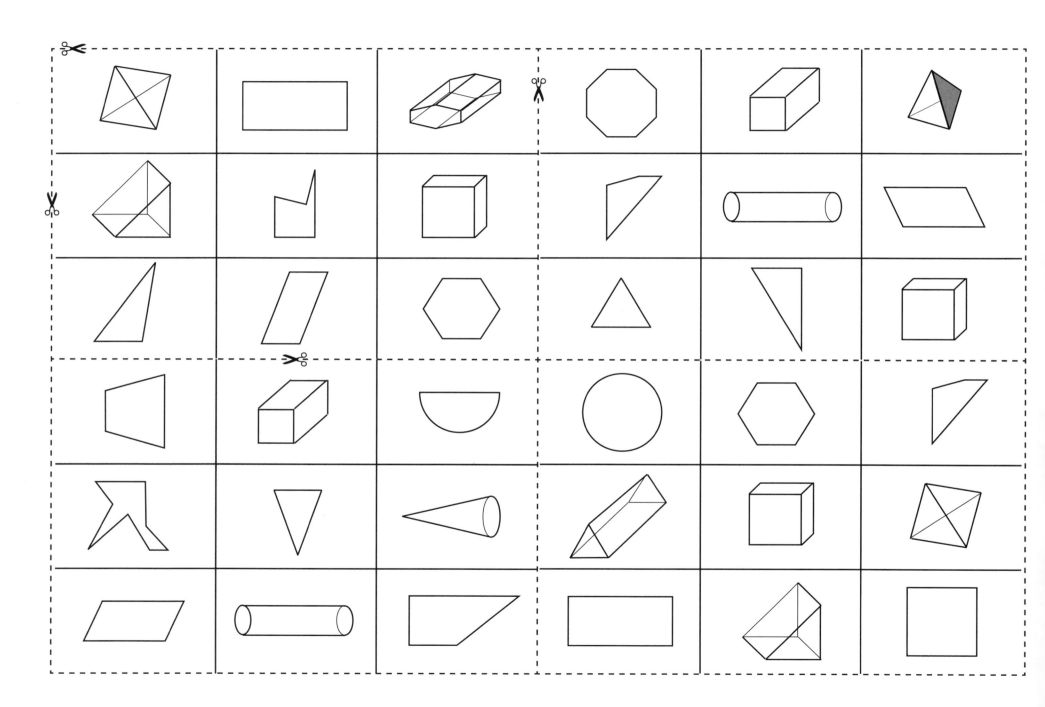

Shape bingo – Game boards

Find a friend

Maths focus: being able to group shapes according to a common property.

A game for the whole class

> **You will need:**
> • Game cards (pages 82–87).

How to play

1. If the number of players is an odd number, the teacher or another adult should play the game. Deal one card to each player.
2. Players are told to 'find a friend' for their card. To be 'friends', the cards must have a common property. For example:
   - Both shapes are quadrilaterals.
   - Both shapes have four sides.
   - Both shapes have straight sides.
3. The players should be encouraged to use mathematical language, but all learners can participate at their own level.
4. When players have found a friend, they should stand with their friend along a wall.
5. When everyone has found a friend, the teacher should lead a discussion on the reasons for each pairing.

Challenge

For a more challenging game, play with other sets of cards, for example a set of number cards. In this case, numbers with the same property can be paired. For example, cards 3 and 23 could be paired because:

- They contain the digit 3.
- They are prime numbers.
- They are odd numbers.

Learners can be challenged to make up additional sets of cards to be used for 'Find a friend' game.

Our cards are friends because both shapes have equal sides.

Find a friend – Game cards

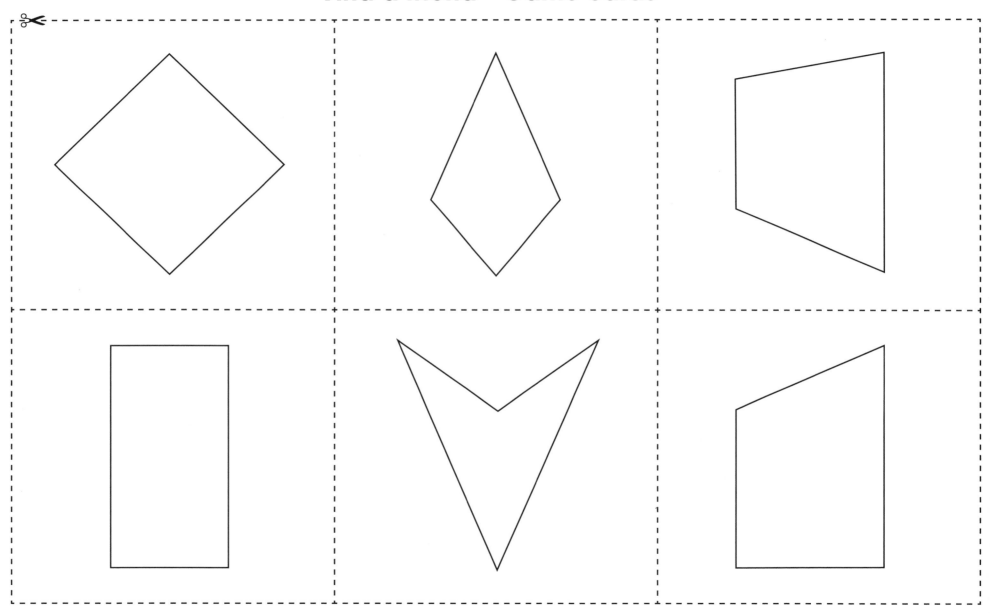

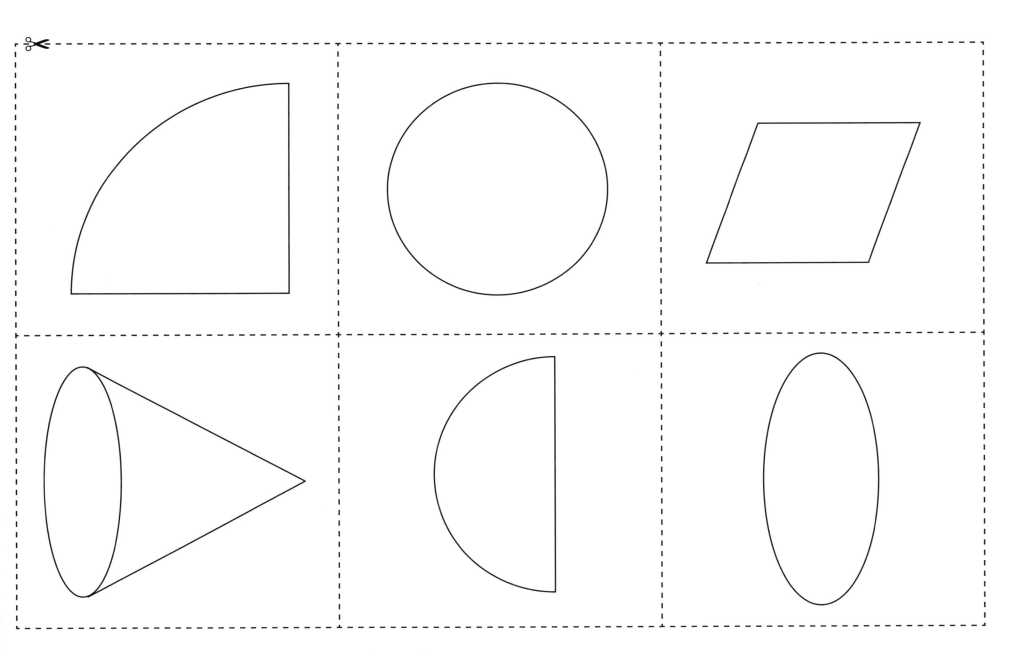

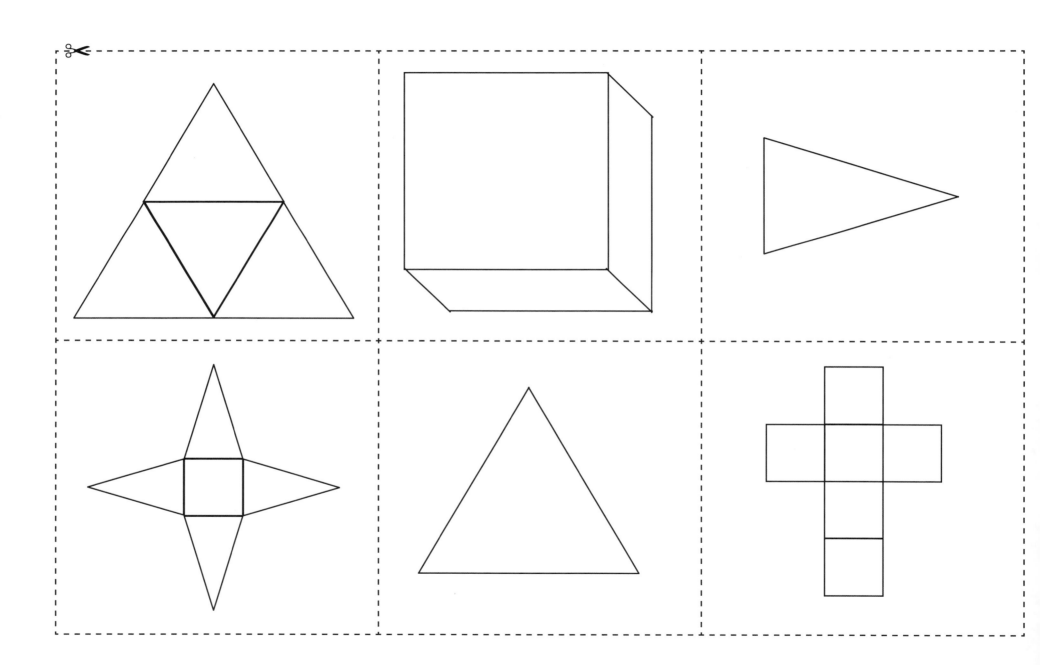

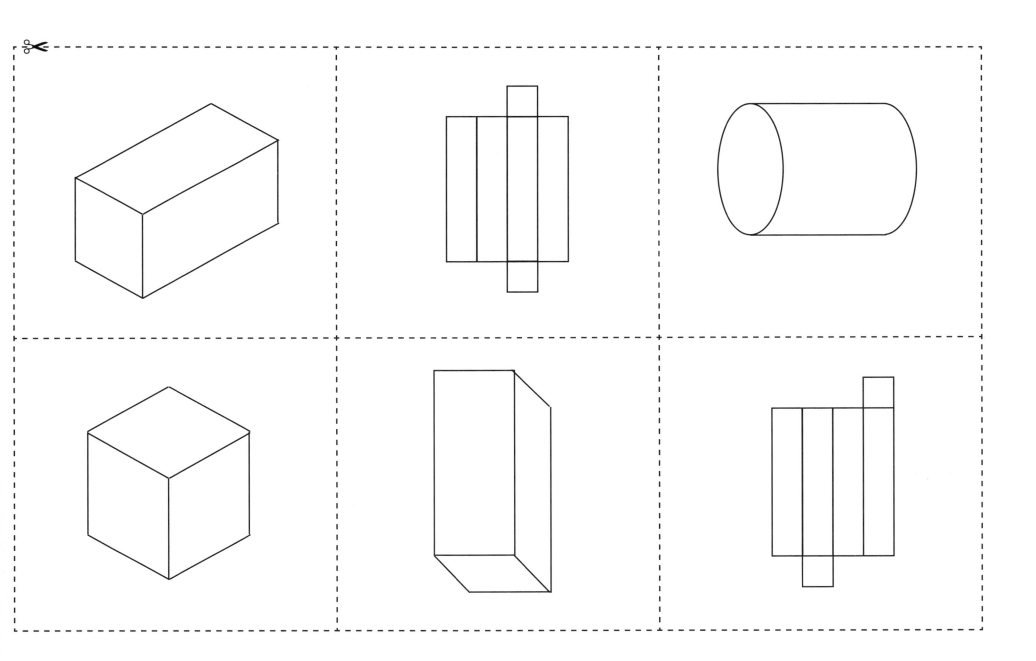

Find a friend – Game cards

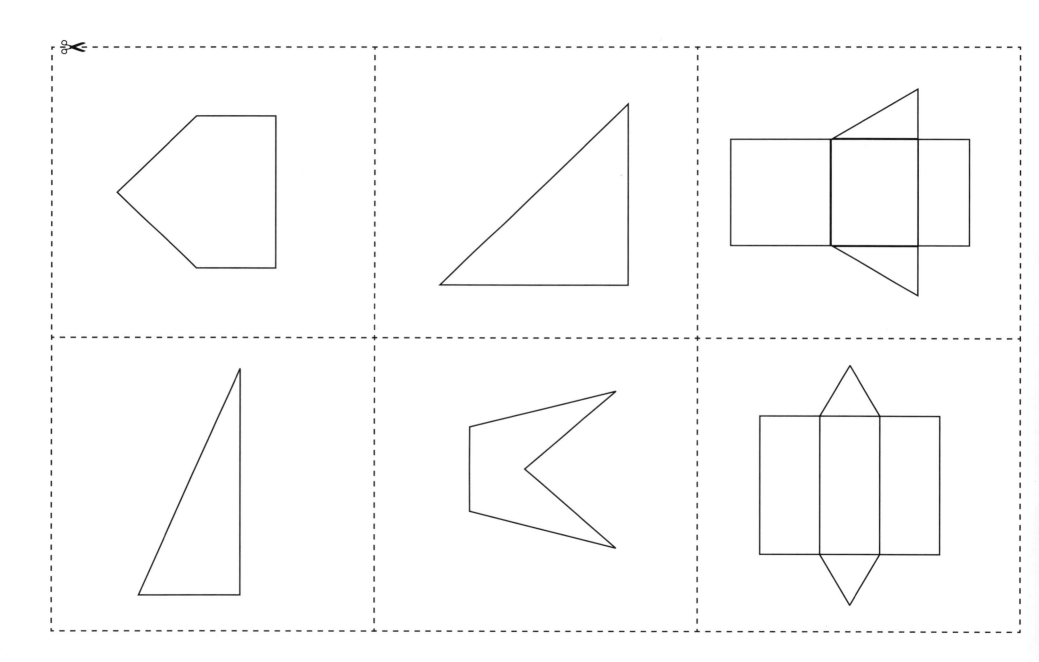

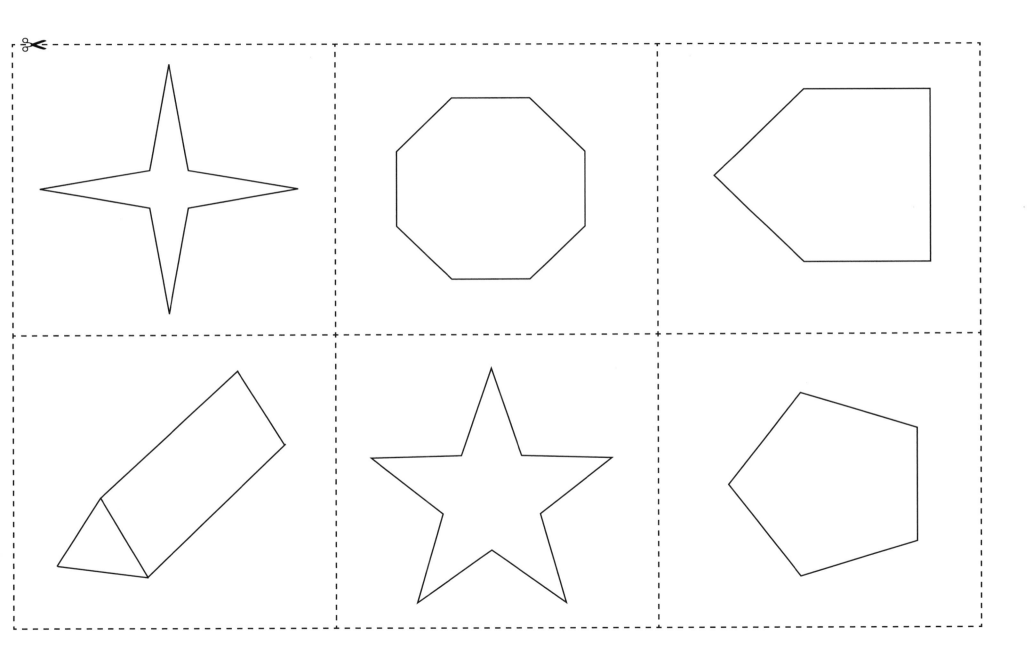

Find a friend – Game cards